DON'T TAKE OUR WORD FOR IT!

Everything You Need to Know About Making Word of Mouth Advertising Work for You

Godfrey Harris

THE AMERICAS GROUP
Los Angeles

Some have asked about the title of this book.
It comes from the opening phrase—
Please, Don't Take Our Word For It...—
of a thought that expresses the essential dynamic
of word of mouth advertising:
...Let Our Customers Speak For Us.

DON'T TAKE OUR WORD FOR IT!

Everything You Need
to Know About Making
Word of Mouth Advertising
Work for You

Godfrey Harris

1st Printing—June 1998
2nd Printing—August 1998

The Americas Group
9200 Sunset Blvd., Suite 404
Los Angeles, California 90069-3506
U.S.A.
☎   + (1) 310 278 8038
℻   + (1) 310 271 3649
EM   hrmg@aol.com
WWW AMERICASGROUP.COM

ISBN:
0-935047-24-7

Library of Congress Cataloging-in-Publication Data

Harris, Godfrey, 1937-
    Don't take our word for it! everything you need to know about
making word of mouth advertising work for you / Godfrey Harris.
      p.   cm.
    Includes index.
    ISBN 0-935047-24-7 (alk. paper)
    1. Word-of-mouth advertising.   I. Title.
HF5827.95.H37   1998
658.8--dc21   97-47481
                                                                   CIP

Printed in the
United States of America by
KNI, Inc.

Cover Design By
Jamie Pfeifer

TABLE OF CONTENTS

PART ONE—
UNDERSTANDING
WORD OF MOUTH ADVERTISING

PART TWO—
BUILDING
WORD OF MOUTH PROGRAMS

PART THREE—
TECHNIQUES OF
WORD OF MOUTH ADVERTISING

7

NOTES

FOREWORD

After studying word of mouth advertising
techniques for nearly 10 years,
I am now convinced
that it deserves to be considered
a marketing tool of equal importance to
media advertising, public relations, and
product presentation.

While many business people readily
recognize word of mouth as a factor in the
growth of their activities,
very few have actually
created programs designed to
stimulate discussions about them.

Moreover, we know of no university courses
and no regular seminars
teaching word of mouth techniques—
and we know of no business or organization
that consistently engages a consultant or
employs a marketing specialist
for the specific development of
word of mouth programs.

This book offers a chance for its
readers to become pioneers in using
their talents and their skills in the
development of word of mouth programs —
something that well could be the
most effective, least expensive
marketing tool available.

Godfrey Harris

ALSO BY GODFREY HARRIS

Concentration
  (with Kennith L Harris)
The Ultimate Black Book—2nd Edition
  (with Kennith L Harris)
How to Generate Word of Mouth Advertising
  (with Gregrey J Harris)
Promoting International Tourism—
  1st & 2nd Editions (with Kenneth M. Katz)
European Union Almanac—1st & 2nd Editions
  (with Hans J. Groll & Adelheid Hasenknopf)
The Panamanian Problem
  (with Guillermo de St. Malo A.)
Mapping Russia and Its Neighbors
  (with Sergei A. Diakonov)
Power Buying
  (with Gregrey J Harris)
Talk Is Cheap
  (with Gregrey J Harris)
The Fascination of Ivory
Invasion (with David S. Behar)
The Ultimate Black Book—1st Edition (1989)
The Panamanian Perspective
Commercial Translations
  (with Charles Sonabend)
From Trash to Treasure
  (with Barbara DeKovner-Mayer)
Panama's Position
The Quest for Foreign Affairs Officers
  (with Francis Fielder)
The History of Sandy Hook, New Jersey
Outline of Social Sciences
Outline of Western Civilization

INTRODUCTION

This is the third book in a series on word of mouth advertising we began some seven years ago. The first book, *Talk Is Cheap,* discussed how word of mouth advertising could be carefully engineered to work effectively for various businesses. The second book, *How to Generate Word of Mouth Advertising,* offered more than 100 individual "recipes" for the implementation of word of mouth programs.

This book, *Don't Take Our Word For It!,* is a summation of all that we have come to learn about word of mouth advertising from the research we have done, the programs we have created, and the seminars we have conducted. Part of that learning has involved how people deal with new ideas on a subject they thought they already knew. To help them focus afresh, this book has been divided into three principal parts:

1. Understanding how word of mouth really works—in favor of something or against it—and when this form of advertising is actually appropriate and when it is not.

2. A compendium of newly created, as well as carefully refined word of mouth programs designed to be used by various sectors of the economy.

3. The major techniques we recommend to make word of mouth advertising meaningful and effective in any circumstance.

We came to the subject of word of mouth advertising quite by accident. It happened while driving with a client in Washington, DC. As the taxi slowed for a traffic light, we spotted a bus shelter poster with a picture of the Governor of West Virginia perched on the edge of his desk. The Governor was dressed in standard blue suit, white shirt, and red tie; an inevitable American flag appeared behind him. The legend on the advertisement read something like: "The people of West Virginia welcome you." My client was involved with governmental support for tourism. "Who would drive all the way to West Virginia based on that?" I asked. "Bet the Governor is coming to town and some staffer was looking for a way to improve his recognition. Typical. Most people with power over spending tourism dollars waste them; they have no real clue how to encourage people to visit a location or get them to use a facility."

The client seemed intrigued by my little speech. "What exactly would you do?" he asked. "Easy. We'd focus on building word of mouth comments so that one visitor couldn't wait to tell a friend, relative, or associate about a particular place." We knew from dealing with a lot of professional travel people that conversation brought more people to a destination than all the paid advertisements combined—and at a fraction of the cost. But paid advertisement is highly visible and can be very satisfying for those paying the bills. (During the 1998 Super Bowl, for instance, ads were selling at more than $1 million per minute to some of America's largest companies. Yet subsequent surveys indicated that only an average of 15.6 per cent of the viewers could identify any single advertiser during the telecast.) The client asked us to send him a memo on how a word of mouth campaign could be developed. He wanted to discuss the idea with his political colleagues.

"Sure," we said. But when we started to work on the task, we found that most people assumed word of mouth was a matter of good fortune. They seemed to believe that positive word of mouth occurred spontaneously and that to interfere in the natural order of things would be tantamount to tempting fate and usurping the role of the gossip gods. Virtually nothing had been written on how to *stimulate* people into talking about a service, product, or event. While we found a lot of anecdotal evidence that word of mouth *worked* in various situations and some academic research that looked at the *impact* of word of mouth comments, there were simply no detailed case studies of orchestrated word of mouth campaigns that had benefited their sponsors.

We later discovered why. Most advertising agencies earn a commission on the value of the advertisement they place for a client. Buying air time can earn up to 15 percent on a placement. Putting the same time and effort into creating an imaginative word of mouth campaign, however, might earn an agency relatively little in comparison. Although they couldn't deny its importance, we think most agencies simply decided they would adopt what we have come to call the tooth fairy defense—that word of mouth happens by magic, rather than by careful planning, original ideas, and artful implementation.

The paper we wrote for our client became a virtual suggestion box of what we thought might get people talking about a particular destination. Along the way, we created a number of word of mouth ideas that on reflection were more suitable to businesses outside of the hospitality industry. The total collection—and more that we added as we got deeper into the subject—became *Talk Is Cheap*. In the book, we divided our thinking on word of mouth advertising into six broad themes. We suggested that when entrepreneurs *listened* and *watched* their customers react to an enterprise—as well as *probed* them for specific ideas on what was right and what was wrong with that enterprise—they would learn what people said about the business and what changes might be needed to significantly alter the text of their conversations. We also advised entrepreneurs to find a way to empower their customers by offering the customers something to give someone else—*meaningful information, a reward, a surprise of some kind*—as a way to to stimulate conversation about the enterprise.

Talk Is Cheap was an enormous success. It went through multiple printings in the United States and is still selling because of references to it in other books and how-to tapes. Foreign language versions eventually appeared in Spanish, Russian, Hungarian, and Indonesian alongside other English language editions published in Britain, Malaysia, and India. Business people all over the world were soon learning how they might make word of mouth work for them. We, in turn, began giving seminars to business groups on our ideas and consulting with individual companies on different word of mouth programs that might meet a particular need. Others would write or call us with a specific problem and ask us which of the ideas in *Talk Is Cheap* we thought would work best for them.

These experiences led us to prepare a second book on the topic of word of mouth advertising—one filled with *specific* program ideas. We found that most people didn't have the time to spend on *why* word of mouth advertising might work or the energy to design their own programs; what they really wanted were step-by-step explanations—virtual recipes—that allowed them to take ideas from the pages of the book and put them to work on the lips of their customers.

The result was *How to Generate Word of Mouth Advertising*. It, too, has been translated and published into a number of languages. The ideas in that book were divided into the principal *techniques* that make word of mouth advertising particularly effective for business. We advised readers on what they could give away and how to do the commonplace a little differently in order to be talked about. We again suggested a number of ways to empower existing clients with something of interest to potential customers, and we offered ideas on how to convert negative experiences into positive conversations.

This book is the culmination of all of our thinking on word of mouth advertising to date. It presents a host of new ideas that have developed since our previous books and thoroughly reworks the best of what we have presented before. We wanted this book to be a virtual encyclopedia of everything we have learned about the topic as well as everything we think anyone needs to know to make word of mouth work effectively for them. We hope we have succeeded.

Godfrey Harris

April 1998
Los Angeles, California
USA

Dedicated
to all those who have
contributed their
thoughts and time
to helping make this
definitive book on
word of mouth advertising
as comprehensive
as possible.

PART ONE

UNDERSTANDING WORD OF MOUTH ADVERTISING

WHAT IS WORD OF MOUTH ADVERTISING?

If it isn't between people who know each other in some way and it isn't direct, it isn't word of mouth.

Word of mouth advertising* involves direct communication about a service, product, business, or event between individuals** who have had some experience with the item and know or have something in common with the people they tell about it.

The strongest evidence, perhaps, of word of mouth advertising*** at work occurs whenever information about a religious apparition begins to circulate. Reported sightings of the image of the Virgin Mary, for example, build from one person to another, with those individuals telling still more people until huge crowds materialize in a matter of days. Thereafter, newspapers and television cameras are attracted to record the phenomenon and assess reactions, increasing recognition of the event among an even larger community.

Despite its descriptive name, some "word of mouth" commentary about services, products, businesses, or events passes from one person to another by other than oral communication:

- *Body language*—a gesture, a movement, even clothing are all now recognized as important ways to communicate an attitude about a given service, product, business, or event from one person to another.

- *The Internet*—EMail, chat rooms, bulletin boards, and interactive WEB sites have become a very

---

* Because word of mouth advertising can be successfully used to promote commercial businesses, government agencies, not-for-profit organizations, or self-employed individuals, we often use the generic term "enterprise" to encompass all of these institutional forms.

** Although some banks have pointedly started to refer to their customers as clients—and some professions and industries prefer to call the public they serve patients or patrons—we use all of these terms interchangeably.

*** Unless we are talking specifically about negative word of mouth, most of our comments involve positive word of mouth advertising.

efficient, inexpensive, and unbelieveably rapid way to "talk" about products and services with others. But the Internet is a sometimes difficult medium to use where word of mouth is concerned. Human speech is modified and amplified continually by facial expressions, hand gestures, and physical movements. We interpret as much meaning from what we observe as from what we actually hear. That insight is missing on the Internet despite crude keyboard symbols—called *emoticons*—that some use to suggest a joke—:)—or express shock—:^0.

- *Symbols* can serve as important word of mouth transmitters. *USA Today* describes a grandmother who traded her Mercedes-Benz for a civilian version of the Army's HumVee all-terrain vehicle. A real estate agent, she posted her company's logo on the doors. "Now she can't make a move in [her small town] without everyone noticing"—and talking about who may be buying and who may be selling through her.

- *Letters*, the traditional alternative to conversations when communicating something to someone else, now have the same kind of immediacy as conversation when transmitted by FAX.

Don't be confused. If the talk—oral or written, personal or electronic, actual or symbolic—isn't between people who know something about each other and isn't directly between them, it *isn't* word of mouth. Remember, it generally takes about fifteen seconds to decide on a dentist—and fifteen years to find out whether the choice was the right one. As a result, most people feel that talking to friends, relatives, and colleagues is a better way to choose that dentist than looking through the Yellow Pages for the largest ad.

Because of the power of word of mouth advertising, simulated examples of word of mouth comments—for example, a concocted quote from a fictious person—have been seen in the last few years. If people have nothing in common, have no personal experience with an item, or have no reason to discuss a particular product, service, business, or event with each other, it really isn't word of mouth.

A final point: Just because someone is talking about a product, service, business, or event does not mean that someone else is listening—or concentrating—on that discussion. If the two sides are not engaged together, word of mouth is not actually happening. So we repeat the definition in the opening paragraph of this chapter:

Word of mouth advertising involves direct communication about a service, product, business, or event between individuals who have had some experience with the item and know or have something in common with the people they tell about it.

TRADITIONAL ADVERTISING V. PUBLIC RELATIONS V. WORD OF MOUTH

Each fulfills an important—but distinctly different—role in disseminating information about a service, product, business, or event.

Traditional advertising requires the involvement of paid media to carry a message—newspapers, magazines, television, radio, direct mail, billboards, and so forth. Public relations reaches the public through much of the same media with information about a product, service, or event using available editorial space or time.

Word of mouth is different. It involves all of the same information carried in traditional advertising or accessible through public relations, but it relies entirely on one individual passing that information directly to another person. Here is an example of how the three work:

- If a concert promoter buys newspaper space to urge other businesses to help sponsor a free concert, that is *advertising*.

- If other businesses learn of the opportunity to help sponsor a free concert through a newspaper article, that is *public relations*.

- If the CEO of one business tells the CEO of another business about the advantages of becoming one of the sponsors of a free concert, that is *word of mouth*.

These differences recently became apparent when Apple Computer, Inc., named a new public relations firm and a new advertising agency as part of its marketing team. Because no one has yet invented the position of word of mouth counselor, none has been appointed by Apple. That's a shame since Apple has perhaps the largest army of loyal customers of any company in the world. That army, once equipped with the appropriate programs and given the proper support, could be mobilized by an experienced word of mouth specialist to help return some of the market share Apple has lost in recent years. (We actually suggested that Apple appoint a word of mouth specialist. See our letter reproduced, in part, at p. 165.)

THE DIFFERENCE BETWEEN A REFERRAL AND A WORD OF MOUTH COMMENT

Whenever we need to pay an invoice denoted in pounds, marks, or francs, we contact Ruesch International. They prepare a check for us in the foreign currency and we send them a US dollar check to cover the costs involved. It turns out to be a fast, efficient, and low-cost way of financing our activities abroad.

About a year ago, we received a needed sterling check from Ruesch, along with a reprint of an article written by the president of the firm. We skimmed the stuffer and noted that it was essentially preaching to the choir. It was describing the benefits of dealing with foreign companies in *their* currencies. We wrote to the company saying that "your customers already know the value of dealing with Ruesch International, that makes them customers. But these customers might be your best sales representatives for [talking about] the value of your services to others." We gave Otto Ruesch, the firm's president, two suggestions for a word of mouth campaign:

- Reproduce a miniature "buck slip" (distribution indicator) in the corner of the paper on which the article is reproduced. "Then in a cover note [encourage] your current customers to send the article on to someone else in international business so that they would have the benefit of your wisdom and experience."

- "You might be able to increase [your customer's] knowledge and reward them for loyalty at the same time by giving them [something] covering a different area of business." We suggested giving customers *two* copies of a handy reference book—one for the customer to keep and the other to send to a colleague.

Eventually, Ruesch's vice president for development gave the ideas short shrift—"we appreciate your suggestions, but will not be utilizing [them] at this time." No reason, no explanation. The NIH (Not Invented Here) brush-off would have been okay if the vice

Referrals occur out of the goodness of the customer's heart; word of mouth generally results from some kind of stimulation.

president for development had previously exhibited some understanding of the crucial difference between a customer *referral* and a *word of mouth recommendation*. She said that Ruesch is "utilizing every opportunity to encourage referral business," something she clearly thought is the same as word of mouth. We explained the difference to her in this way.

> Referrals, for the most part, are *passive* events—given by customers only when someone in need of help asks for assistance and then generally without a reward to the individual making the referral. Word of mouth recommendations, on the other hand, are the result of *proactive* programs where customers are specifically rewarded for talking about a product, service, business, or event.

> In the case of Ruesch, the customer reward we suggested was getting to look good while helping a friend, colleague, or associate understand foreign currency transactions (such as passing the Ruesch article along) or having a handy reference book to send to someone that would evoke a thank you and could start a conversation about where the book came from.

Having decided against rewarding their customers in a word of mouth program, how does Ruesch expect to get its customers to make referrals? The vice president for development told us they were conducting "a corporate-wide incentive contest" among their *employees*. Having preached to the choir with an article on things customers already knew, they were moving on to giving prizes to the employees for referrals that they expected their *customers* to make.

Referrals happen by chance; word of mouth happens by direction. We summed up the difference in the headline of a flyer we prepared for a client:

What is the difference between...

A REFERRAL, A RECOMMENDATION, AND A REFERENCE?

NOTHING*

*unless one of them brings in more business
by becoming a word of mouth comment.

WHY IS WORD OF MOUTH ADVERTISING SO EFFECTIVE?

Ever wonder why television personalities such as Oprah, Rosie O'Donnell, and Regis and Kathy Lee are so popular with the general public? While no one fully understands the chemistry between performers and their audiences, we suspect that one reason for the enormous following of these talk show hosts is an ability to discuss private events and private thoughts so openly and so guilelessly. They seem to say whatever pops into their heads in a way that makes members of the audience feel among their closest confidants.

The next time you happen to catch one of these programs, try to determine if our impression matches your own reaction. Aren't you drawn to the program more by the personality and conversation of the host than by the guest stars appearing or the topics being discussed? Professor Robin Dunbar, an anthropologist at University College, London, theorizes that human speech evolved among women sharing time and space doing grooming activities in primitive societies. He believes that the reason an overwhelming proportion of human conversation today involves gossip about relationships is because this information tends to provide insights into motives and morals—and this allows us to predict the behavior of others.

We think the same kind of intimacy in conversation makes word of mouth advertising so valuable. Since you know the person who is discussing a service, product, business, or event, you have a reliable way to gauge how you may react and how it may impact on your own needs, desires, and expectations. It is the same kind of intimacy that works so well for charities. When people are asked point blank by friends and relatives for a donation on behalf of a particular charity or cause they are supporting, most people find it hard to deny the request. Oh, there may be a question about how much to give or the eventual use of the proceeds, but generally some contribution is made out of friendship, kinship, or loyalty to the

In brief, word of mouth works because it connects on a personal level.

person requesting the donation.

This is the same power that word of mouth delivers:

It is trust, faith, and knowledge of the person doing the communicating that carries so much weight on behalf of a product, service, business, or event.

As a result, the best word of mouth campaigns try to bring something personal to bear on the discussion about a product, service, business, or event. One way to engender this feeling of intimacy is to let people know about you or your business in a way that you might tell a close friend, sibling or partner. You don't have to reveal everything to the people who you hope will carry the message about your product, service, or event, but what you do reveal needs to be something honest and open—why a sale didn't work, why a campaign failed, why a product is popular, why you chose the hours you are open, or what plans you have for the future.

The very act of talking is an important social statement. For example, *New York Times* columnist William Safire believes that talking "is a New Yorker's way of showing friendship, especially to strangers."

Of course, there may be another reason why word of mouth has proven so effective in recent days. It is best reflected by a little license with the words of a prayer made famous by Robert F. Kennedy:

Please grant me the Serenity to
accept the things I cannot change,
the Courage to change
the things I can,
and the Wisdom to hide
the bodies of the
Salespeople I had to kill
because they really bugged me!!!

The prayer indicates that traditional selling through paid or commissioned sales staff has lost favor with customers. It suggests to us that word of mouth—when it is driven by interesting, personal, revelatory, and honest information—may a worthy substitute.

REVERSE WORD OF MOUTH PROGRAMS

In reverse word of mouth programs, individual customers—rather than a business— initiate the program. In these cases, the individuals are trying to benefit a business, product, or event in return for some special favor or privilege they seek. While not common, these programs have a place in understanding how word of mouth can work in the marketplace.

To demonstrate how reverse word of mouth can work, we received an EMail message from a cousin complaining that "99.99% of restaurants [serve] only diet Coke or Pepsi—no diet un-cola drinks." He hoped that we would join in a crusade to change this lamentable situation. We said that if we were leading this crusade, we would equip everyone in our army "with a few little cards...to leave with the cashier" or a manager of a restaurant that failed to have un-cola diet drinks available. We noted that "the power of the printed word to reinforce the power of word of mouth is a very potent force."

To demonstrate the concept, we asked whether our cousin would be prepared to engage in a little research for us. We said we would print a dozen or so cards for him to carry in his wallet, if he would leave them at appropriate places and later check on whether the card had done any good.

You can see a reproduction of the card on the following page. It turns out that few restaurants changed their buying habits to accommodate Alan Davidson's request. Most of the restaurants, it seems, are chain operations, and their buying is centralized at some distance from individual stores. As a result, these stores have no authority to buy on their own. Either the buyers at headquarters are not sensitive to the customer requests, or they were unwilling to create another inventory item to track. From our standpoint, it was an example of how many people pay lip service to the importance of word of mouth

Customers volunteer to spread the word about a business in return for special services.

advertising, but are really oblivious to its power and potential. Either way, the restaurants are now losing business because Mr. Davidson reports that he and his friends tend to frequent only those places that have now stocked what he wants.

Note a feature we designed into the card: We included a name and address so the manager could determine authenticity of the request if he thought it was some marketing campaign organized by a soft drink distributor. By suggesting that he would bring his friends, Davidson was offering to initiate a word of mouth program for the restaurant.

TO:	RESTAURANT MANAGER	ALAN DAVIDSON BUSINESS NAME
FROM:	ALAN DAVIDSON	STREET ADDRESS CITY, STATE
SUBJECT:	NON-COLA DIET DRINKS	(800) 555-0100

WE THOROUGHLY ENJOYED OUR MEAL IN YOUR RESTAURANT, BUT WE HAVE ONE SMALL SUGGESTION FOR IMPROVEMENT. WE LIKE NON-COLA DIET SOFT DRINKS WITH OUR MEALS. DO YOU THINK IT MIGHT BE POSSIBLE TO ARRANGE WITH YOUR BEVERAGE SUPPLIER TO PROVIDE A STOCK OF NON-COLA DIET DRINKS FOR YOUR CUSTOMERS? WE WOULD APPRECIATE IT AND WE KNOW A NUMBER OF OUR FRIENDS WOULD AS WELL. WE LOOK FORWARD TO OUR NEXT VISIT...AND TO BEING ABLE TO TELL OUR FRIENDS HOW KIND YOU WERE TO RESPOND TO OUR REQUEST.

LOOKING AT WORD OF MOUTH ADVERTISING REALISTICALLY

People do not talk about topics that are far from their mutual experience with others. While movie critics in a social situation might discuss the movie business, non-critics generally would not discuss films with casual acquaintances without some specific spark to steer the conversation in that direction.

We observed this the other evening when we went to dinner at our neighbor's house. The hostess had invited the folks that live on both sides of her home and those directly across the street—five couples in all. The conversation never lagged...from local restaurants we like, to the price of recent home sales, to the strange habits of some of the absent neighbors. But, interestingly, no one talked about a local election for the city council of Los Angeles coming in two days, an election that had generated an intense amount of mailed literature, telephone calls, and even walking canvassers. One person did mention receiving a particular piece of campaign literature, but not even that was a strong enough lead to generate conversation about the relative merits of the candidates.

What's the point? If you pay attention to what people talk about and when, you realize that word of mouth does not generally happen spontaneously and does not happen just because someone offers a superior product or service. If you don't specifically stimulate it, it is likely not to occur. Just as most people are afraid to ask for a sale for fear of rejection, so most business people are afraid to ask for a mention of their product. But if they don't, who will?

It takes the same mentality to create a conversation about something as it does to sell it. People have to believe it will do others some good. In short, if you are not prepared to sell a product, you cannot be prepared to stimulate people into talking about that product.

> If word of mouth is not stimu-lated, it probably won't occur.

TALK ABOUT PRODUCTS OR PUBLIC ISSUES DOES NOT OCCUR SPONTANEOUSLY

People are usually ready to talk about a product or service when something interesting or unusual draws their attention to the topic.

Several years ago, our consulting firm did a study for a California-based political action committee after a close election in California. Although the group that hired us had won, they had spent a lot of money in the process and were anxious to find ways to save money the next time they had to defeat a rent control issue. We were asked to look at the question of *when* people had actually made up their minds on the ballot question and the *basis* for that decision. We developed a brief questionnaire and an interview script and went looking for voters a week later.

We were not surprised to find that most people reported devoting very little time to making up their mind on political topics. The people told us that they generally ignored all the campaign information as it poured down on them—the mailings, flyers, newspaper articles, television interviews, campaign appearances, fancy brochures, outdoor billboards, and the like. While they may have been aware of them and noted aspects of various items on a superficial level, nothing apparently sunk into their consciousness.

Then, those who eventually voted admitted that something happened to arrest their attention—a chance word on the radio, a flash of recognition of something they saw, a moment without other concerns, a point of confusion about some aspect of the issue. It was at that instant—and that instant only—that our message had a chance to get in and to influence their thinking. We called it the windowshade effect. At some point during the campaign—but never at a time that could be predicted or planned—the shade covering their consciousness on political issues would lift sufficiently to allow them to focus on a newsclip, read a document, consider a comment, or think through an issue.

Once the individual fit that tiny sliver of information into a pattern he or she accepted or balanced it against some other factor of importance, the mind was made up for or against the issue. Within a flash of the moment that the windowshade had lifted, it was pulled down again; the game was over. The decision had been made.

Everything else done during the remainder of the campaign became reinforcement for the decision that the voters had reached. In fact, we were surprised to learn that they watched, read, and listened to campaign material—whether for or against the position they had decided on—with much more intensity and thought *after* making up their minds, than before.

We think conversations about products or services work in exactly the same way. People simply don't talk naturally about the power of their oven cleaners or the purity of the sugar they use. To get products like these—as well as political subjects—into the conversation requires prompting; once the issue is raised in an appropriate context and once the other person has his mind in gear, the windowshade will raise sufficiently to consider the points being offered. He or she will either accept or reject the information, based on the trust the individual places in the person offering the information and how the information itself connects with the person's other predilections. Once the information has been assimilated, the windowshade will likely close. Traditional advertising is likely to reinforce the decision—and may offer an opportunity for the individual to pass along what he or she has just learned—but it is not likely to change that viewpoint.

Word of mouth, then, is not a sponstaneous event; it is as dependent on the way the conversation is prompted and a person's receptivity to new information as the top speed of a car is dependent on the size of the engine and the conditions of the road.

KEY STIMULANTS TO WORD OF MOUTH ADVERTISING

They'll start talking if you surprise 'em and exceed their expectations.

Word of mouth advertising is at work whenever two people discuss a service, product, or event that one or the other has experienced.

As we have noted, individuals have a hard time launching into a discussion of their favorite aspirin or the relative merits of gas vs. electricity. Because of this, most successful word of mouth advertising results from some type of *stimulation*.

To stimulate one individual into communicating positive word of mouth comments about a service, product, or event to another, be sure to employ one or more of these key forces:

- *Surprise*—Something that occurs suddenly, unexpectedly, or out-of-the-blue is generally successful at generating spontaneous comments.

- *Difference*—Doing something differently literally becomes a conversation piece. While the competitive bar is continually being raised in the battle for attention, difference is the stuff that people talk about. For example, one cellular company in the Los Angeles-area offered a limited number of free weekend calls as an incentive to use their service; its competitor promptly fired back with free calls at all times to the customer's *home* number, and so on.

- *Expectations*—Whenever a service, product, or event goes beyond what customers expect—and becomes different, unusual, or special—it usually creates conversation. By the same token, whenever a service, product, or event falls below expectations, it can generate negative word of mouth comments.

- *Authenticity*—If the comment comes from real people using real products in real life situations—and is transmitted directly from one person known to another—word of mouth will work successfully.

- *Remarkable*—Tom Clancy, in his book *Executive Orders*, writes that the fictional new US President

Jack Ryan would soon have "a custom-designed chair fitted to his own back by a manufacturer who performs the service for free and—remarkably—without public fanfare." Oh, really? Clancy, perhaps, forgets the power of word of mouth advertising. Rather than an overt advertisement announcing that the firm works for the White House, the mythical orthopedic chair manufacturer need only quietly mention to clients that one of his chairs had been made for the President or had just been delivered to the Oval Office to garner all the endorsement and testimony anyone would ever want! Washington lawyers, forever giving cut-rate fees or forgiving them altogether, extol the positive buzz received among potential corporate clients wheneve they represent political players enmeshed in high-profile scandals.

No matter how successfully a word of mouth program is stimulated, *timing* still plays a key role in its effectiveness. People worrying about their kids, concerned about meeting a deadline, or late for another appointment may be too distracted to react to new information no matter how it is presented. We were reminded of this during the commemoration of Moscow's 850th Anniversary in 1997. A lot of time and money had gone into sprucing up the city and planning the events. It was hoped that millions of potential tourists and investors would see it on international television. But just days before the commemoration's inaugural events, Diana, Princess of Wales, died in a car crash. The world's attention was riveted on every facet of the tragedy. Then two days before Diana's London funeral—and only one day before the opening events in Moscow—Mother Teresa passed away in Calcutta. That set off yet another wave of memories and mourning. No one had a mind for Moscow's celebrations.

Timing, of course, can always work the other way. Take a recently released biography of Bela Lugosi. Interest in and discussions about the life story of the Hungarian actor received a boost with the fortuitous release of a US postage stamp honoring Lugosi's famous role as "Count Dracula." On the other hand, a movie on James Dean's life has not been shown in theatres despite publicity about the movie. In the film, Robert Mitchum portrays George Stevens, the man who directed James Dean in *Giant.* Mitchum died after the Dean project was completed, making the Dean film Mitchum's last. Interest in one of Hollywood's most enduring stars, rather than the story of the life of one of Hollywood's most famous icons, may prove to be the factor that brings the film to the public.

When timing works against a word of mouth program, the rule is to repeat as many aspects of the program as possible. While Moscow could not repeat its 850th Anniversary, others have the luxury of repeating information often enough and in enough different ways so that some part of their message about a product or service may get through to allow people to hear, see, and process new information from those they trust.

WORD OF MOUTH THROUGH STATISTICS AND AS A RESULT OF RESEARCH

Formal research and anecdotal data both suggest that word of mouth advertising is a key factor in the marketing of many products and services.

Word of mouth advertising is continually being validated by academic research as well as marketplace experience. It is hoped that the few examples noted here are sufficient to justify programs undertaken by businesses new to the task of trying to stimulate their customers into becoming the most effective element of their sales department.

• Chemical Bank in New York bought a traditional advertisement to proclaim: "...our clients are our single most reliable" means of acquiring new accounts.

• One study some years back noted that homemakers rank word of mouth as the "single most important influence on a decision to try a food product." Campbell Soup, as an example of this, reports that people purchase a new soup 90 percent of the time if someone has personally recommended it!

• In a survey of security companies, 30 percent of their new customers came directly from the recommendation of an established customer.

• Telemarketing works, in the words of one marketing executive, because "you get a chance to speak directly to people...many people like to have people call them...some people just can't say no to someone on the phone." If that proves true for unsolicited discussions with strangers—and is more than seven times (!) more effective than direct mail—think how it might work when a relative, friend, or associate starts talking about a service, product, business, or event.

• Remember that word of mouth advertising usually starts with an established customer. Making that customer more powerful, knowledgeable, or important—in the hope of generating word of mouth comments—also strengthens the customer's prestige. That's important, since Harrison Publishing Co. reports that "it costs five times more to acquire a new customer than to retain an existing one."

- The power of *personal* communication between people known to each other seems even more important now that behavioral scientists have found that first impressions are based 60 percent on *appearance*, 33 percent on the way people *speak*, and only 7 percent on what they actually *say* in a conversation.

  This finding was confirmed when researchers found that 38 percent of the people in a study reacted to voice cues (same words said softly or forcefully, with an accent, involving poor grammar), while fully 55 percent of the people responded to gestures and movements (same words, same voice cues, but with physical movement, facial expressions, and hand gestures). The lesson is that we can spend too much time worrying about *what* a person will say about our products or services, when it is *how* the person says it that really counts.

- Most small businesses rely on word of mouth advertising as a matter of survival—clearly, they cannot afford to do as much media advertising, direct mail programs, or special promotions as their larger competitors. Despite this, we have found that most small business people do not know how to stimulate word of mouth so that it serves as a tool for expansion. Too bad, since CNN reports that 70 percent of family businesses do not get to a second generation of ownership, and 80 percent fail to reach a third generation. We suspect that the odds of survival would be greatly improved if more family businesses learned how to employ some of the techniques described in this book.

- The US Census Bureau reports that response rate to its forms was 85 percent in 1970, but dropped to 70 percent in 1980, and 65 percent in 1990. The Bureau sites skepticism about government, busy lifestyles, and the tendency to throw away anything that looks like junk mail. The cost of a recipient taking action on a letter is $2; the cost of having to send someone to the door to get the form completed is $12. If nothing else, this difference suggests the enormous cost of other forms of commercial communication compared to word of mouth advertising.

- A tourism consultant in England calculates that 70 percent of theme park business arises from positive word of mouth comments, while 80 percent of the problems of the same industry can be traced to negative comments.

- Studies conducted a few years ago by a Washington research firm concluded that only 4 percent of dissatisfied customers provide feedback on what bothers them, but some 80 percent discuss their negative experience with others.

- As if to prove our theory that most business people believe that word of mouth occurs by chance, a 1997 survey of publishers listed fifty-seven ways that participants used to market their books, tapes, and CDs, but word of mouth was not among them.

In a major 1997 ad campaign to introduce eleven new television shows to prospective viewers, the ABC network used an "It's Okay to Watch TV" theme. Huge yellow billboards suddenly appeared in major markets emblazoned with the ABC logo and short messages such as:

- *Scientists say we use 10% of our brain. That's way too much.*
- *8 hours a day, that's all we ask.*
- *It's a beautiful day, what are you doing outside?*

The *Los Angeles Times* reported that the campaign generated "the desired buzz," but wondereded whether it would "succeed in generating more viewers?" The question is out of place. One step at a time. First, get the conversation started, then move it to a specific subject. No doubt, ABC's ads on television got the conversation under way.

WORD OF MOUTH ADVERTISING MISUNDERSTOOD

Many businesses say that they can only exist because of word of mouth. While they strongly believe in the concept, they really don't understand when it works or how it can be stimulated.

- Most non-stimulated word of mouth comments arise when existing customers are asked by curious non-customers about a service, product, business, or event. "Where did you get that?" or "Who do you use for plumbing?" Technically, these questions lead to *referrals*. Word of mouth is something that starts with a happy customer talking about a product, service, business, or event with someone who might be able to benefit from the same thing.

- A radio station in Los Angeles continually urges listeners to tell someone about the station if they like what they hear. Nice thought, but not a word of mouth program. People simply don't talk about non-personal, non-public subjects without some prodding or a reward system. When was the last time anyone told you about his or her long distance carrier or favorite brand of dental floss?

- Word of mouth is not a magic promotional bullet. It cannot make up for a poor product, bad service, or the need for accurate information. Traditional media, the Internet, even a recorded toll-free telephone message are much better at conveying location, starting times, and prices, for instance, than word of mouth.

- The movie industry believes strongly in word of mouth, but generally does very little to stimulate it. The one notable exception involves the effort to become the most watched film on any given weekend, believing that fact alone will generate news, induce talk, and somehow result in people flocking to see the film. Given the mythic significance that first weekend ticket sales have attained—and the amount spent to achieve a num-

Because of its perceived power, many people claim word of mouth is at work for their products when it really isn't.

ber one ranking—some studios cheat by releasing early *estimates* of what they say the final numbers will show. Movie people seem to believe that neither newspapers nor television stations will offend a major advertiser by refusing to carry the "news" they generate and that if they are grossly wrong in their estimates, the correction will never catch up with the exaggeration.

• Finally, word of mouth is not a form of speech. It has nothing directly to do with how articulate customers are or how quick they think on their feet. It has only to do with the positive or negative nature of what they eventually say or indicate to their friends, relatives, and associates about a product, service, business, or event.

FAUX WORD OF MOUTH
PROGRAMS

Because word of mouth about a service, product, business, or event, by definition, arises in a conversation between two individuals known to each other, it suggests a level of honesty and frankness that is often missing in traditional paid advertisements or news releases. As a result, advertisements often try to simulate word of mouth commentary. While immitation may be the height of flattery, legitimate word of mouth programs ought not end up unintentionally looking and sounding like the fakes that abound.

Here are some examples of those fakes:

- Newspaper and magazine advertisements that proclaim strong word of mouth support for a product often quote the comments of ordinary people. If the people are not known to the readers, it is not legitimate word of mouth commentary.

- Theatrical producers use this technique all the time for new shows. They film the excited, positive reactions of people as they emerge from a theatre and use the clips in their television advertising. Lacking a connection between those quoted and those being influenced—other than perhaps a similarity in age and maybe taste in the clothes or accessories worn—there is no basis to trust the endorsement. It may be worthwhile advertising, but it won't be word of mouth at work. Movie executives anxious to mimic word of mouth comments, often lace their advertising with banner-line phrases such as: "Get a Peek at the Movie Everyone is Talking About"—whether true or not, whether they know or not, whether it matters or not.

- *The Wall St. Journal* recently reported on a company located in Morristown, New Jersey, that employs "placement" agents to recruit the leaders of civic, educational, athletic, arts, and support groups to distribute samples, coupons, and other freebies to those in their orbit. The idea is to create a "buzz" about the products behind the give-

The aura of authenticity that surrounds word of mouth commentary leads many to borrow some of its powerful status under false pretenses.

aways. Real word of mouth? *The Wall St. Journal* thinks so. We don't. One critic of the methodology believes that anything so clearly tainted by a corporate hand would turn the public off. We don't agree with this comment either. We simply say that word of mouth about a product occurs from direct contact between two people known to each other. The person distributing the coupons or giving away the free samples is not endorsing the product or even talking about it. In most cases, apparently, he has never even used it! He is merely serving a mailroom function by distributing something of value to his or her associates. Such an activity might help get word of mouth started eventually, but it would not constitute word of mouth in itself.

- Recently, we have noticed a trend over the fax and in the mail to simulate a word of mouth message. A "handwritten" note addressed to "Sue," "Mike," or some other common name is "written" on what purports to be a reprint of an article or advertisement. One recently came to our office. It was an advertisement for a stop smoking product called "Oxy Quit." All the usual confidence giving statements were included—ten-day guarantee, doctor-formulated, clinically-tested, all-natural, no cravings. What intrigued us so much was not the typeset words, but how the ad itself was scrunched down toward the bottom portion of the paper in order to leave a generous amount of room for the fake word of mouth message the sender wanted the recipient to read: "Cindy" it said in mock handwriting, "This is the program we were talking about. It's Amazing! Give it a try and pass this on to someone you know who needs it." The message ends with a very familiar: "Call me later. -Melissa-" Nice try. No one in our office smokes; no Cindy has ever worked for us. The only Melissa we know calls herself "Lissie." But the dead give away to the sham was the tell-tale at the top of the fax identifying a mass distribution service: "FROM PANASONIC FAX SYSTEM."

- Many, many companies borrow on the familiar idea that talk is the cheapest form of advertising—it is a theme we ourselves used in the name of our first book on word of mouth advertising (*Talk Is Cheap*) and a theme familiar to anyone involved with word of mouth campaigns. When phone companies use it—as AT&T did to introduce low rate Customer Appreciation Days in 1992 ("Talk is Even Cheaper!")—they are merely playing with words that have resonance in the culture, rather than building better understanding of word of mouth.

- Another subtle form of playing on word of mouth techniques occurs in advertisements using before and after photographs. One heavy advertiser of body makeovers embellishes the photographs with a headline: *I thought I'd always be fat!* Nice touch, but the words are printed without quotation marks and are clearly meant to imply that they are those of the women pictured when they aren't.

- Finally, Charles Schulz, the renowned creator and illustrator of the *Peanuts* cartoon strip, had another take on the topic. Charlie Brown wonders how Lucy gets business at her psychiatric help booth without advertising. Lucy is shown shouting: "All right, where is everybody? Let's get over here right now!" Linus, observing the scene, notes that she has "the best kind of advertising there is...WORD OF MOUTH!"

LOST OPPORTUNITIES TO EMPLOY WORD OF MOUTH

Because of its remarkable power and minimum cost, no business should pass an opportunity to build word of mouth for the long term even if it means losing some short term business.

Word of mouth advertising is generally more effective and certainly a lot cheaper than traditional advertising. Yet, we have noticed countless times when companies have missed opportunities to generate word of mouth advertising for themselves:

• Take a new car dealership in Los Angeles seeking additional work for its service department. "Free loaner car and free car wash with each service" the radio announcement proclaimed. Nice offer. But it would have been better to use the loaner car as the public enticement to try the dealership—that is a big enough deal—and leave the free car wash as a "surprise" bonus for the owner to discover for himself when retrieving his vehicle. The fact that someone did something extra for a customer—without making a fuss and without asking for thanks or payment—is exactly the kind of thing a husband would tell a wife, a wife would tell a friend, and a friend might tell her boss or even a company transportation manager.

• Computer software companies could do the same thing. Instead of describing *all* aspects of a program in its advertisements and on its packaging, let the user discover some of the neat things about the product for him or herself. It is much more likely that having done so, the owner will want to share those discoveries with a friend and therefore build more sales at less cost for the software company than a continuation of an *all-inclusive* traditional advertising campaign.

• Missed opportunities also arise when individuals oversell a product. We have all had the experience of friends seeing a movie and raving about it, and then being disappointed when we saw the movie ourselves. Our expectations were raised so high by the description that they became virtually impossible to meet. *Underwhelming* people is a way of exceeding their expectations.

- Anyone who voluntary sings a company's praises ought to be preserved in bronze. Too often, though, they are not. We saw a letter to the editor in the travel section of the *Los Angeles Times,* apparently unsolicited, extolling a tour company for rebating $150 as its response to the writer's complaint about a scheduling problem. That tour company ought to have a way—a focus group, advisory committee, newsletter, or some other device—to use the letter writer's obvious support with potential customers. We once wrote to the Postmaster General praising the Postal Service for delivering 1000 of our first class letters to radio stations across the country in less than twenty-four hours. "I'd be happy to provide some word of mouth commentary," I wrote, to offset any correspondent with "an opposite experience." The form letter response indicated my letter was never read or that the suggestion was totally beyond anything the postal service had ever contemplated. Shame. It was another example of a lost opportunity to use happy customers as the strongest element of a selling effort.

- Hong Kong reported a severe decline in tourism following its return to China in July 1997, blaming an area-wide economic crisis that began in August, choking smoke from Indonesian forest fires, and, finally, a deadly new strain of avian flu. While Hong Kong authorities contemplated a traditional media advertising campaign to reverse this trend, we thought a special word of mouth program aimed at new target segments within established markets and themed to a message that the dangers are exaggerated would be a better, less expensive, and, in this case, even faster approach.

- Kenneth Turan, film critic for the *Los Angeles Times,* has recently lamented the fact that too many movies are being made. He explains that Hollywood has "created a machine that must be fed, screens that must be filled....Like a shark, Hollywood must continue to keep moving or it will die." He points out: "The question is not how many [movies] you've seen, [but] how many have you heard of." We think there is an even more fundamental point: If you've seen or heard of a movie, what will get you to talk to your friends and relatives about it?

WORD OF MOUTH CAN BE VERY SLOW

As in the classic race between the tortoise and the hare, the prize does not always go to the swiftest; it can go to the more cunning.

When movie producers dream that the buzz about a film will send its popularity soaring, they are thinking in terms of days and weeks, not months or years. If initial word of mouth comments on a film are enthusiastic, producers expect traffic into the theatres to increase the very next weekend.

But such quick results are not generally an attribute of word of mouth advertising. Like good cheese, it requires a little aging to achieve its best results. A good example is how some Japanese women have started using Valentine's Day in a different way. It seems that Japanese men are generally better at expressing love with their wallets than with their words and tend to shower girlfriends with showy gifts. If a relationship ends—and a woman wants to be done with all the reminders—she can sell the unwanted goods at a Tokyo department store's annual Valentine's Day Love Liquidation Sale. The store takes $1 on each sale, and no item may be sold for more than $100. The event grows larger each year through word of mouth—among those who want to be rid of gifts and those who want expensive items at bargain prices.

In the same way, talk helped fur products make a fashion comeback after years of exile in the back alleys of political incorrectness. Saga Furs of Scandinavia, an international fur marketing organization, demonstrated the kind of planning, patience, and perseverance that pays off in word of mouth advertising. Saga invited young fashion designers to fly to Copenhagen to learn the intricacies of working with fur in their collections. Some three to five years later, the results are evident in increased prices at fur auctions and expanding use of fur in garments, along with an avalanche of articles in the fashion press about the beauty, suitability, and warmth of real fur. The buzz among the customers of high fashion is that it's all right once again to buy and wear fur.

In the book trade, the slow pace of word of mouth used to be one of its *strengths*. Publishers sent books to stores, a few people would read and discuss them (usually bookstore employees with customers), sales would increase steadily, and eventually an ever-growing market for subsequent titles in the same genre or from the same author would build. Not today. Big publishers now answer to bankers and stockholders; they are not only gripped by what one writer described as a "burning impatience" for instant best sellers, they deal with equally large multi-store mega-chains that tend to hire people only capable of stocking shelves, completing a credit card transaction, or making change. People who love books and love to talk about them are not considered cost effective. Word of mouth, so important to the growth of publishing in the past, is no longer an important factor in marketing most new books. But some would note that shrinking sales and burgeoning returns are the result. It will now be left to small and independent publishers to use word of mouth techniques to bring growth and change back to the industry.

Finally, different age groups within the population tend to be involved with word of mouth differently. "Grumpy Old Men," a film with an obvious appeal to older audiences, had a "slow and steady" box office history. According to Bob Harper, president of Fox marketing, this segment of the population doesn't "rush out opening weekend as a rule; they wait to hear what their friends say about it." It is an important lesson for everyone using word of mouth advertising. One program may not be suitable for all customers; incentives may have to vary depending on who is expected to carry the message for a company.

WHEN WORD OF MOUTH MAY NOT WORK

Don't rely on word of mouth comments to sell short term events or brand new products, destinations, or services.

As sure as we are that word of mouth advertising is the most effective and least expensive form of information dissemination—when properly stimulated and continually adjusted to changing conditions—we are also sure that it is not appropriate in every circumstance or for every type of organization. For example:

- **Short term events** cannot live on word of mouth alone. Take a visit of the famed Bolshoi Ballet to Los Angeles. The company offered three different ballets over its eight-day stay in the city. By the time each of the three was first performed, there was virtually no time available to allow word of mouth comments to percolate from someone who had seen a performance to someone who might enjoy the next one. By the time recommendations could be made or schedules arranged, the company was not performing that ballet or had left the city. As a result, companies such as the Bolshoi— or businesses such as catering firms or funeral homes—need to learn how to sustain positive word of mouth comments over long time gaps.

- **New products or destinations** cannot be talked about by anyone until they are tried by *someone*. Most people are at their most enthusiastic about a new product or place when they are enjoying it or soon after they first try it. As a result, while introductory programs are never suitable for word of mouth advertising, a coordinated *follow-on* campaign immediately after a new product launch should be.

- **New services** are only susceptible to word of mouth advertising when initial users have some experience with all aspects of the service. Allow people some time to use a service and then test all of its aspects before asking them to speak to colleagues, friends, or relatives about it.

- **Affordability** plays an important role in the success of word of mouth advertising. A colleague of ours attended a week-long financial seminar. He couldn't have been more pleased with what he derived from his experience. He had no doubt that the same seminar would be of great benefit to us. We would probably agree. But unfortunately the tuition was $6,500, an amount we simply did not have available at the time to devote to a project of this nature.

- **Exclusivity** can play a similar role to affordability. Products, services, or events limited to people with the appropriate eligibility—by virtue of membership in a particular club or organization, by meeting specific background or age requirements, by having the necessary educational credentials—are generally not good candidates for word of mouth. Conversations either end up as preaching to the choir or with people who cannot use the information discussed.

- **Differences** in taste, style, values, outlook—even among relatives and close friends—are impediments to word of mouth working. No amount of enthusiasm expressed for the acting, direction, or cinematography of an X-rated film, for example, is likely to get someone with strong views on the debilitating effects of pornography or the declining moral fibre of the nation to rush out to buy tickets.

- **Desire** can also play a role. We overheard two couples in the supermarket discussing a sourdough dip one had tried. It sounded awful to us. It led us to conclude that unless there is a predilection for a product, unless some groundwork has been laid to heighten interest, or unless a person is predisposed toward something, the word of mouth can fall on deaf ears.

- **Privacy considerations** can also work against word of mouth. Some men in Britain are notorious for refusing to reveal their tailors; some hostesses would never dream of talking about their caterers; individuals being treated by a psychiatrist or attending group therapy sessions may be reluctant to name the professionals involved. While there are several ways, such as through the Internet, to make word of mouth work under these kinds of circumstances—or for products/services that treat very personal medical needs or problems—the rule is reinforcement for our belief that *random* word of mouth is a myth.

- **Lack of attention** can beat the best word of mouth programs. As former NBA player and coach Bill Sharman once said of today's professional players: "Just because you have something to say doesn't mean anybody is willing to listen." Nothing could be truer of word of mouth as well.

NEGATIVE WORD OF MOUTH

Negative word of mouth comments are as easy to prevent as positive word of mouth is to create.

Negative word of mouth is when people discuss what is wrong with an enterprise, rather than what is right with it. Just as positive word of mouth can be stimulated by competent management to increase business, so negative word of mouth can be generated by inattentive management to ruin a business.

Most negative word of mouth results from sloppy service, poor quality products, or unsafe conditions. Sometimes, of course, it is totally unfair—the result of misinformation or inaccurate reporting. All of it, however, can be fixed by management...if only they knew it was out there and were attentive to providing a solution early enough. The problem is that negative word of mouth does not always appear as a slam-bang complaint. Most of it, in fact, arises when a customer is disappointed. Rather than suggesting a solution, the customer either stays away from the firm or sticks pins in its reputation by sharing nasty comments with friends, relatives, and colleagues.

- We tell the story of a young couple forced out of their rental unit by a broken water pipe and being put up in a nearby hotel by their landlord while repairs were being made. A friend visited and was impressed with the hotel's facilities. "The beds are terrible," the wife moaned. "I'd never stay at one of these places again." When asked if she complained to the hotel manager or even asked the front desk for a new mattress, she said she didn't want to make trouble. But her negative word of mouth comments could prove more troublesome to the hotel chain than she would ever imagine.

- We are also reminded of the all too common occurence at restaurants when diners find the soup too salty or the vegetables still raw. While they know they ought to send the faulty items back, their waiter has disappeared in the kitchen or they are running out of time before the movie starts or the baby sitter has to leave. So they say nothing at the restaurant, but let their friends know that it would be a cold day in hell before they returned for another meal at that restaurant.

We have a simple cure to stop negative word of mouth. It is to ask questions—the right questions—before negative comments can do any damage. It is also to reward the customer for responding to the questions with a generous gift. Most hotels—and restaurants for that matter—teach members of their staffs to ask patrons: "Was everything all right?" While a nice gesture, it is the type of question that intentionally invites a positive response. Most people mumble yes or just nod at this question, even when everything isn't all right. It takes a lot of energy to articulate a problem or express a concern. So we recommend specific questions that help the patron to respond honestly to the question or open up with another thought.

Hotels should try variations of: "Do you need more lighting in your room? Is the heating system making any noise?" Restaurants might ask: "Can I bring you some more hot rolls? Was the meat sliced too thinly for your tastes?"

If the person has been forthright in his comments or deserves some form of compensation for a problem, then an official above the individual doing the questioning needs to appear to make the award. In the case of the hotel chain, *two* complementary weekend rooms at another facility—one for the couple with the complaint and one for them to give to a friend to use might turn a negative feeling into a positive experience. The restaurant management could do the same for the people with the salty soup or raw vegetables: A $20 gift certificate for them to use the next time they come in and a $20 gift certificate for them to bring another couple with them on a subsequent occasion. (NOTE: While most coupons have expiration dates, these shouldn't.)

Don't you think when those kinds of rewards are given for others to use that it would spark a conversation between the people involved? Isn't it possible that the negative thoughts would be automatically converted to positive feelings about the establishment?

Remember that most positive word of mouth arises when a customer's expectations are exceeded, and most negative comments come when a customer is disappointed by something that occurs. These two thoughts can be expressed by the following formulas:

Level of Expectation + Added Benefits = Postive Word of Mouth

Level of Expectation - Unfulfilled Benefits = Negative Word of Mouth

WORD OF MOUTH IN
OTHER CULTURES

It is a strong force in many countries.

In America we say that information passing from person to person is heard on the "grapevine." In Haiti, communication between people is often referred to as *telediol*—literally, mouth television. Others in the Caribbean have an even more evocative phrase for word of mouth. They call it Radio 32, a reference to the number of teeth in the mouth. In Panama, people talk to each other on *Radio Cocina*, or kitchen radio. But it is much more than just gossip; in some cultures it is more important than newspapers, radio, or television, all of which may be controlled and manipulated by the authorities as a means of communication. In fact, one prominent Panamanian notes that *Radio Cocina* "was the most effective instrument during the Noriega years to get news in[to] the street."

Several years ago, my wife wrote an open letter to the people of the Soviet Union and sent it to the Editor of *Pravda*, then the principal newspaper of the Communist Party. She asked people to support the programs of Mikhail Gorbachev for fear that something far worse might replace him. The year was 1990, and Gorbachev had just introduced his program of *glasnost* (openness) and *peristroika* (restructuring). As if to prove that the society was now open, *Pravda* published my wife's letter translated into Russian along with her picture (taken from a résumé she had submitted to provide credentials for her point of view) and our home address. A few weeks went by, and a great avalanche of letters started arriving, many opening with the phrase, "You probably won't receive this, but..." Because most of the letters reached us in Russian, we had to engage a translator; my wife felt that every letter deserved a personal answer and each got one. We later learned that the letters received from the United States were the talk of many small villages and among many family groups. Soon more letters arrived, now from people who had never read the original piece in *Pravda*. Amazingly, they continue to arrive to this day as people hear about this concerned, interested person in the

United States.

The power of word of mouth was so strong in Russia—and could be put to such good use as the country changed from a command to a demand economy—that a translation of our first book on the topic, *Talk Is Cheap*, sold out within days of its appearance. Eventually editions of that book and our second book, *How to Generate Word of Mouth Advertising*, appeared in England, Mexico, Indonesia, Hungary, Malaysia, and India with still more translations—including Russia—now on the way.

WORD OF MOUTH ADVERTISING CHECKLIST

Word of mouth programs involve aspects that are personal, remark-able, and special.

The line between various forms of information dissemination is very narrow. Traditional advertising can borrow from elements of word of mouth just as word of mouth can benefit from the output of a public relations campaign.

To better understand the key elements of a word of mouth advertising prgram, we have devised a checklist of questions. If the answers all come out yes, you have a true word of mouth program under way.

- Is information about a service, product, business, or event designed to pass directly from one person to another?

- Does this program involve something sufficiently unusual, surprising, or different that it is likely to cause one person to remark spontaneously to another about it or give another person an incentive to look at it for themselves?

- Does the program involve a gift or special privilege that can be awarded by an old customer to a new one on your behalf to insure that what does not arise from spontaneity comes from common courtesy?

Finally, a bit of realism before turning to descriptions of some actual word of mouth programs that can be employed in various sectors of the economy and with various types of businesses. Note that nothing works all of the time and nothing will work on every potential customer in the same way. As a result, target each program to attract just a few new customers. If it achieves that goal, it will reward your effort. If it achieves more, it will encourage you to design a fresh program for a point in the future when you again need to call on your established customers to help you grow.

PART TWO

BUILDING WORD OF MOUTH PROGRAMS

AN EXPLANATION OF THE PROGRAM CATEGORIES

This section is devoted to presenting a variety of word of mouth programs. Rather than organize these programs by theme or by technique—as was done in our previous books on word of mouth advertising—we have arranged the programs by their primary suitability to various sectors of the economy. While some programs are designed for a specific industry, please note that many can work in other sectors as well. As a result, review all the programs, even if the sector seems outside of your personal concerns.

- ALL SECTORS
  Programs that we believe can be beneficially adopted for use by any commercial enterprise, non-profit organization, or individual practioner. *

- BASIC INDUSTRIES
  Programs that are particularly suitable for agricultural, mining, and manufacturing enterprises.

- NON-PROFIT ENTERPRISES
  Programs aimed at assisting the work of charities, foundations, governmental agencies, political parties, labor unions, and other activities where profit is not a goal.

- PROFESSIONAL FIRMS
  Programs designed for lawyers, doctors, architects, engineers, consultants, designers, and others who work primarily from an office setting.

- RETAIL BUSINESSES
  Programs suitable for any store, mail order house, restaurant, or other outlet that deals directly with the general public.

- SERVICE BUSINESSES
  Programs designed for craft and trade specialists—plumbers, barbers, and electricians—as well as travel and transportation companies.

- WHOLESALE BUSINESSES
  Programs for those businesses that deal primarily with other businesses rather than with the general public, including multi-level marketing groups and networks.

---

* Most of the programs have been designed for organizations—businesses, non-profit groups, governmental agencies—to use in reaching their goals. But individual practioners need to know how to generate word of mouth about themselves for their own benefit. For example, actors need to generate word of mouth about their talents; assistant directors need to promote themselves into their first full directing job; freelance photographers, independent copy editors, portrait artists, and other specialists who sell their skills on their own can use word of mouth techniques and programs to generate jobs. If the programs discussed in the *All Sectors* section or under *Professional Firms* cannot be adapted to an individual's needs, please see the discussion in Section III on word of mouth techniques.

INVITE CUSTOMERS TO COMMENT

ASKING CUSTOMERS TO ARTICULATE THEIR FEELINGS CAN BE ENOUGH TO START THE WORD OF MOUTH WHEEL TURNING.

The following ad has appeared in Sabena's in-flight magazine:

Did you have a good flight?

We try our best to make your journey
as pleasant as possible.
If you have any comments on our service
- complimentary or critical -
please write to :

■ **Customer Relations Manager,**
SABENA HOUSE
Box 4
1930 Zaventem

sabena ⁰

ALL SECTORS

We think it is always a good idea to invite customers to speak about their good or bad experiences. Once you get someone articulating what they liked or didn't like about a product, service, or event, it is easier for them to talk to others. If it was a good experience, you are on the way to having positive word of mouth generated; if it turned out to be a bad experience, you have taken a major step toward diffusing the hostility and anger the person may have felt before he talks with a potential customer.

All businesses can benefit from Sabena's good example. Not all businesses, of course, have a magazine. Posters or banners, flyers or mail inserts can serve the same purpose. A few thoughts, though, to strengthen the word of mouth impact of the concept:

• In Sabena's case, we would have recommended inclusion of a telephone, fax, and/or EMail address in the ad to greatly increase the chances that a passenger would actually communicate an opinion.

• We would have embellished the request for "any comments" into a much more specific search for ideas:

ANY COMMENT IS WELCOME, BUT YOUR THOUGHTS ON OUR GROUND ARRANGEMENTS, FOOD AND BEVERAGE CHOICES, PERSONNEL ATTENTIVENESS, INFLIGHT READING MATERIAL, OR BAGGAGE HANDLING WOULD BE PARTICULARLY WELCOME.

Providing hints is a particularly helpful technique if you are planning changes and understand how to use customer feedback.

- We would always suggest a generous gift certificate, discount coupon, sample product, or other reward for *anyone* taking the time to respond to a request such as Sabena has made.

Final thought. Like a money-back guarantee, you won't get many responses to your invitation. But just showing that you care enough to ask creates a positive impression with customers.

MAKE THEM THINK!

TREAT YOUR CUSTOMERS WITH INTELLIGENCE AND RESPECT, AND THEY WILL TREAT YOUR BUSINESS NEEDS IN THE SAME WAY.

Our publishing colleagues were recently asked to participate in a survey conducted by something called the Book Publishing Research Institute. What caught their attention was not the standard questions asked—how many employees, how many books are you going to publish next year, what element of the industry concerns you the most—but the simple, effective way the sponsors enticed recipients into participating.

ALL SECTORS

- The outside envelope had an overprint:

> **"WE REQUEST YOUR CANDID OPINION.**
> (A free cup of coffee is enclosed.)"

  Clever. How, our colleagues wondered, could the sender stuff a cup of coffee into a flat envelope?

- Rather than a coupon, a U.S. $2 bill fell out as they unfolded the cover letter. "Can I buy you a cup of coffee," the letter began, "at Starbuck's rates." The letter went on to say that the Institute needed a "<u>candid</u> evaluation of the state of the [publishing] industry and various book marketing practices."

- "Did someone on the staff respond to the request," we asked? "You bet," came the reply. They felt obligated to show their appreciation for what they thought was an innovative, original, and very imaginative approach.

Any business can adopt the same concept as a word of mouth program. Say you would like customers to communicate with colleagues about a service you just performed or describe a product they just bought. Because people are sometimes reluctant to do these sorts of things, merely request the name, address, and phone number of a colleague they think might be interested in the service or product and ask them if it would be all right if *you* called the colleague to discuss it. Put the request in an envelope with the same words the Research Institute used or try: "I'd like to buy you an ice cream." Remember to include a $2 bill or vary it with several $1 bills or even a $5 bill. Ask the recipient to pick up the phone, then and there, to give you the information that would benefit you. Make sure you have a way of recording the information, should the individual choose to call after hours.

You will get the contact you want and your customer will have enjoyed a smile from the letter and the reward from its contents with no harm to anyone in the process.

BUMPER STICKERS
MAKE THEM QUESTIONS INSTEAD OF STATEMENTS!

We have long advocated the use of bumper stickers as an aid to word of mouth commentary. But the messages we have in mind would be different from the typical political slogans and humor seen in America today:

Clinton 96 —Save the Whales —China Out of Tibet—
The Gene Pool Could Use a Little Chlorine

These messages usually only tend to encourage conversations from those who agree with the sentiment expressed; they do not invite the kind of talk that changes minds or creates new business from favorable word of mouth comments.

But the other day we saw our kind of bumper sticker as we drove along the 405 Freeway in Los Angeles. A deep blue Jeep Cherokee had an intriguing message plastered on its high, chrome bumper:

LOOKING FOR A HOME BASED BUSINESS?
1 310 555 0100

When we saw it, we were filled with thoughts as we sped along at 65 miles per hour. Given the value of the vehicle, this person's home based business seems to be treating him well. But if he is in a home based business, why is he in the parade of cars on a freeway just before rush hour? Ah, we mused to ourselves, perhaps it is his wife's car and he is on the way to Los Angeles International Airport to pick her up. We never learned the real answers to any of these questions—and, at freeway speeds, we were never able to write down the exact telephone number to call the company later—but we were impressed with the way the bumper sticker was phrased. As a rule, we believe that a question helps start a word of mouth conversation better than a statement.

We know that many advertising mavens despise questions for fear that they will evoke the wrong answer in the reader. We also know that telephone marketing gurus recommend asking only those questions that draw a yes or positive statement from the respondent. We disagree when it comes to word of mouth advertising. We believe that open-ended questions invite conversation. As such, they are a way to start word of mouth advertising spinning toward a larger audience. Unless the other person's attention is engaged and unless the conversation begins, topics that can lead to increased sales cannot even be broached.

POST-PAID BUSINESS REPLY ENVELOPES

A NEW IDEA FOR BUSINESS COMMUNICATION.

Nearly everyone in retail agrees on the importance of free and convenient parking. There is less of a consensus on the value of 800, 888, and 788 telephone numbers to generate new business, since they also bring a flood of questions and a share of complaints that many retailers like to avoid.

But there is even less agreement on the value of a mail order business paying the cost of postage for its clients. While a substantial portion of businesses include pre-addressed envelopes in their mailings, few pay the postage itself. The reason is cost. If the recipient does not answer the communication, the value of the pre-paid stamp can be lost or used elsewhere. If business reply mail is used, mail actually delivered by the postal service is paid for by the sponsoring business. But that cost is not only substantially more than the cost of a first class stamp, it seems to encourage pranksters to return blank cards or empty envelopes to the sponsoring organization.

We have an idea to solve the dual problem of wasted stamps and high cost business reply systems and get a word of mouth bounce in the process. We call it *Post-Paid Mail.* Here the sender pays for the original stamp, but gets **two** stamps back from the receiving company. In the box where a stamp would normally be affixed, we suggest the following wording: "Double Postage Reimbursed to Sender by Recipient."

The return of double the postage—*two* stamps for one or a *coupon-reponse interntaional*(CRI) for international correspondence—suggests a number of advantages to the company using this new system.

- It offers a business a built-in way to acknowledge the communication from the customer.

- It gives the customer a second stamp to communicate with someone else about the product or service provided...a way to pay for the cost of stimulating word of mouth comments.

- It permits a company to pay for the postage of its international clients.

Double Postage Reimbursed to Sender by Recipient

POST PAID BUSINESS ENVELOPE
DOUBLE STAMPS OR THEIR VALUE RETURNED TO SENDER

**THE AMERICAS GROUP
9200 SUNSET BLVD.—404
LOS ANGELES, CA 90069
USA**

SAY THANK YOU WITH PANACHE

IF YOU SHOW APPRECIATION FOR A REFERRAL OR WORK, DO IT IN A WAY THAT WILL CREATE COMMENTS.

ALL SECTORS

If you are going to thank a client, do it in a way that has a chance to generate comments from others. Listen to this story about a person who has referred her friends and associates to a dentist. One day after lunch she returned to her desk to find an enormous arrangement of flowers waiting for her in a huge vase. These were not your ordinary carnations or roses; these were the tall stemmed, exotic flowers and leaves that generally form the grand arrays in the lobbies of four-star hotels. The color, shape, size, and number of items in the arrangement had people stopping and talking. Here is a sample of how one of those conversations went:

"Melissa, who sent you those flowers?"
"My dentist."
"Your dentist. Boy, he must either be the guiltiest guy on the block or he wants something that you don't want to give."
"He is a she and she just wanted to thank me."
"Thank you for what?"
"For sending so many people to her, I guess."
"You refer people to your dentist?"
"Absolutely. She is always on time for her appointments, she never talks to you while you have all that equipment in your mouth, she never suggests anything unless you really need it done, and she isn't very expensive."
"Sounds like someone I should go to."

Flowers are always a nice way of saying thank you, and, while they may evoke a comment on how pretty they are, they seldom start whole conversations on completely different subjects. This dentist understood, better than most, that to start a conversation requires doing something unusual, something remarkable.

How much did the flowers cost? Probably around $200. As flowers go, that is a lot of money. But as advertisement costs go, it was cheap. Think about it. You can't design and buy display space in a newspaper or prepare, stuff, and mail 500 letters today for that kind of money. And it's not only the money; it's the impact. Had the dentist given her patient a bottle of perfume, no one would have been the wiser. Had she presented a $200 gift certificate for a meal at a fancy restaurant, only her dinner companion would have known. The flowers, on the other hand, were seen by dozens of people, and at least two of them made appointments with the dentist—more than paying for this word of mouth marketing program.

REBATE CASH TO YOUR CUSTOMERS

FIND A WAY TO SEND MONEY BACK TO YOUR CUSTOMERS, AND THEY WON'T STOP TALKING ABOUT IT.

One of the great stories that illustrates why word of mouth is a separate marketing tool involves a firm that makes awnings, upholsters cushions, and creates covers for boat owners. To stimulate conversation, the owner had a rule. If a customer spent more than $1,000 on a job, he would automatically send him a rebate about three weeks after the job had been completed. Here is an example of the kind of letter that he would write:

Date

ABC Repairs
Street Address
City, State ZIP

Dear Client:

We enjoyed working on your boat last month; we hope you are getting as much pleasure from what we crafted for you as we had in making it.

We have a rule at ABC Repairs. If we overestimate the cost of the supplies we use, we think it only fair to share the savings with our clients. The cost of the material used on your job was 15% less than we assumed because of a special discount from the manufacturer.

Please find our check for $22.50 enclosed. We look forward to serving you again in the near future.

Sincerely,

Albert B. Crane
Owner

Here's a simple question. If you received a surprise rebate out-of-the-blue from a craftsman, do you think you might mention it to a friend, colleague, or relative under the heading: Guess What I Got in the Mail Today? You bet you would. If a tailor, lawyer, accountant, car mechanic, or repair shop sent you a rebate long after the work had been completed, do you think you would have a favorable impression of the way the person does business? Do you think his or her name might pop to mind the next time you are asked for a referral?

TABLE TALK

GIVE YOUR CUSTOMERS SOMETHING INTERESTING
TO TALK ABOUT, AND THEY WILL.

ALL SECTORS

Conversation has clearly become an endangered species in the United States. We realized this when my wife and I discovered that a major restaurant chain now uses special paper wrappers to hold their knives, forks, and spoons in place. Each wrapper contains a provocative question that is intended as a conversation starter, perhaps for those more used to watching television or reading than talking while eating.

Here are the two questions the wrappers posed for our table:

- *What is the one convenience you would not want to do without?*
- *What was one of your favorite family dinners as a child?*

Good questions, we thought. They worked with us who are non-stop dinner table talkers anyway. After a moment of thought, each of us answered the questions posed and then we were explaining or justifying why we selected the choices we made. They were the type of questions that both the taciturn and the loquacious could respond to. The wrappers even offered a little encouragement to get diners started, explaining that "you never know what new things you might learn about your favorite people."

Every business can use this idea...slip little conversation starters in with each product, print them on your statements or receipts, stuff them into envelopes with anything sent to customers. Invite them to discuss the topic with colleagues or family over lunch or dinner. But instead of general topics, we urge questions that relate to the products, services, or events that the business promotes. For example:

- If a *wholesale business* dealing in electronic products, ask what the individual considers the most important electronic product?
- If a *retail business* dealing in automobile parts and accessories, ask the individual what feature in his or her car provides the most pleasure?
- If a *non-profit group,* ask what charity seems to do the most good for the most people with the least fuss?
- If a *professional firm,* ask the individual to identify the one government agency that provides the most important service to the citizenry?
- If an *individual practioner,* ask what living person they might want to see cloned if the procedure were to become acceptable at some point in the future?
- If a *political group,* ask if a second Mt. Rushmore were to be carved, who ought to be included as a match for the four Presidents (Washington, Jefferson, Lincoln, and Theodore Roosevelt) now on the original?

LOTTERY TICKETS

PARTICIPATE IN CHARITY DRAWINGS BY GIVING THE TICKETS YOU BUY TO COLLEAGUES AND CUSTOMERS.

If you are asked to participate in any kind of charity drawing, consider buying multiple tickets or books. Look upon the drawing as a chance to develop a word of mouth campaign.

If you buy the books, for example, in pairs, you would have one to give to a customer and one for the customer to give away to someone else. Because books of tickets usually consist of five to ten tickets, you could also suggest to your customers that they share the individual tickets from a book among their staff members or with their suppliers.

We were once asked to assist the Romanian Orthodox Church in Los Angeles with a drawing to raise funds to furnish a newly acquired sanctuary. The tickets were priced at $5 each, but books of five tickets could be purchased for $20—a savings of $5. Although we were involved in organizing the drawing, we decided to buy several books ourselves. We gave the books to clients we had not worked with in a number of years and asked them to pass the individual tickets along to others they know. All were reminded to fill out the ticket stubs and send them in to be eligible for the drawing.

It turned out to be an effective platform to talk to our former clients. As soon as they received the tickets, they called to say thank you, let us know they were excited about winning, and ask why we were helping this church. It gave us the chance to talk about ourselves and our new directions and to seek to recapture their business or make a pitch for the business of a contact of theirs.

 $5 — 5 Tickets @ $20   Sfinţii Arhangheli "MIHAIL şi GAVRIL" Saints Archangels "MICHAEL & GABRIEL" $5 — 5 Tickets @ $20

Win a $2,000 35" Mitsubishi Stereo Television
with an Advanced Picture-in-Picture Feature
as well as many additional Special Prizes.
Raffle will support the Congregation of the
Saints Archangels "Michael & Gabriel" Romanian Orthodox Church
in its effort to furnish a new sanctuary
for its religious services and educational programs.

Date of Drawing: 3:00PM, April 16, 1995 Place of Drawing: At the Church TV Winner to be notified by telephone	*MAILING ADDRESS* Romanian Orthodox Church PO Box 4724 Garden Grove, CA 92642-4724 (714)555-0100	*CHURCH LOCATION* 4102 Hickman Drive Torrance, California 90504

LET YOUR CUSTOMERS TALK— GOOD AND BAD

SPREADING NEGATIVE WORD OF MOUTH COMMENTS ABOUT A COMPETITOR MAY BE A LEGITIMATE BUSINESS PRACTICE.

ALL SECTORS

A tiny shop solely devoted to baking and selling bagels has been a fixture in our neighborhood ever since we moved there more than twenty years ago. The queue waiting to be served has been a traditional Sunday morning meeting place. Where else could you see the most disreputable looking people imaginable—in torn sweats and raggedy shorts, over-coats and baseball caps, bleary of eye and stiff of joint—emerge from the most expensive cars available to wait docilely for some fresh baked bread, while either trying to control some feisty four-year-old or browse a section of the Sunday paper? But recently things changed. The local bagel shop was sold to a regional chain, the location was changed, and prices were raised almost 100 percent. A delicatessen in the neighbor-hood decided to win over the customers the chain was clearly losing. They declared a "Bagel War."

Huge banners proclaimed bagels for 18¢ each, considerably less than the 55¢ the regional chain was now charging. This was not something to be ignored by the neighbors who all fancy themselves to be clever and discriminating buyers—ourselves included. So naturally we bought a few of the less expensive variety to try. They were terrible, tasting more like a stale Parker House roll than a traditional bagel. No hard crisp crust here, just a soft, flakey overcooked coating with a bitter flavor. Three bites and we knew the birds would have a winter treat on the ones we would be throwing out.

It occurred to me that while businesses ought to promote positive word of mouth comments from their customers, there is also nothing wrong with using the principles of word of mouth advertising to generate negative comments about the competition. In the case of the bagel war, I thought the regional chain could do itself an immense favor by buying dozens of the 18¢ variety each morning and inviting people to stop by for *free* bagels and coffee! Inside the shop, we would also post a sign that reads: "YOU GET WHAT YOU PAY FOR!" and serve some of the more expensive variety along side the cheap one.

After a few mouthfuls of comparison eating, I have no doubt that people would be talking about the difference for years to come and perhaps be willing to stand in line once more. Unfair? Not in response to a "war" declared by the other side.

IT'S TIME!

Sometimes word of mouth stimulation can be gentle; offer a good idea, and it will pass from one person's lips to another, generally with credit to the business initiating the idea. Word of mouth stimulation does not have to be as blatant or as obvious as a coupon, card, or other direct message.

For example, any business could send postcards with a reminder for clients to:

- Recharge their fire extinguishers;
- Clear their rain gutters and drains;
- Rotate emergency food supplies;
- Review all medicine labels to remove out-of-date supplies;
- Check the tire pressure on all vehicles,
- Plant vegetables;
- Spray for moths;
- Turn sensitive objects away from the sun;
- Spread fertilizer;
- Defrost a refrigerator or freezer;

or the like.

Here is an imaginery reminder that could be printed on a self-stick label, card stock, or a postcard to send to existing clients as well as potential clients.

Harry The Handyman
[Insert this card behind the light switch plate nearest to your smoke detector. Remove it only *after* you have completed the task below.]

TEST THE SMOKE ALARM BATTERY!

(200) 555-0100

61

CONSIDER THE WORD OF MOUTH VALUE OF WEB SITE ADDRESSES

WITH SPACE AND WORLD WIDE ACCESSIBILITY, WEB ADDRESSES ARE INSTANT CONTACT WITH THE WORLD.

A L L   S E C T O R S

As we have pointed out, the clear hope of word of mouth advertising is that the person receiving information on a new product or service will act on it to the benefit of the company, organization, or individual that provides it. Sometimes, however, the information fails to pass smoothly—a trade name is misspelled, a telephone number has a transposed digit, a mailing address is a little known suburb rather than a major metropolitan name.

We have been impressed with the power of World Wide Web addresses to solve this problem. One word or several linked together provide everything anybody needs to learn key details about a company or product. We now recommend that companies—seriously interested in promoting word of mouth commentary about themselves, their products, services, or events—establish a definitive single web address that identifies all of their activities. Not only can a web address encompass as many as twenty-two characters—versus the seven of a toll free telephone number or nine of a vanity license plate—but once a person has accessed the site through the Internet, an almost endless stream of accurate information can be conveyed to the person about all manner of products or services.

Some thoughts to keep in mind as you apply for your individual web address. Use the name of the business, product, service, or event that is either familiar to the public or one that you hope to establish in the public's mind. The web address of The Americas Group, the publisher of this book, for instance, is:

www.americasgroup.com

Although it looks a little strange all in lower case lettering and without a space, we think adopting the full name of a company works fine. We think familiar abbreviated names such as www.nytimes.com for *The New York Times* is easy to remember and access. On the other hand, we note that 20th Century Fox chose www.anya.com as the web address for its film *Anastasia*. We think the Fox marketing people erred in selecting a nickname for the web address because it is spelled differently from the film and would be harder for people to remember. We also feel a wholesale electric company, Green Mountain Energy Services, made a mistake in choosing a *sloganeering* website—www. choosewisely.com. In our view, cute sayings or difficult word combinations are hard to remember and harder still to pass along to others.

DO SOMETHING SPECIAL FOR SOMEONE ELSE

GIVE YOUR CLIENTS SPECIAL PRIVILEGES THEY MIGHT NOT OTHERWISE RECEIVE.

ALL SECTORS

Last Christmas, one of my sons flew to Washington, DC, with his wife for the wedding of a teaching colleague. I asked if they had any plans besides the wedding festivities, and both said they had never been to the White House. It took a little effort to connect to someone who could help in arranging tickets for one of the special tours, but I managed it. They said it was one of the highlights of their trip.

Everyone has access to something special, if not directly, then through contacts. Think where your connection might be and how you could, on occasion, ask on behalf of someone else. It might be a backstage pass at a concert, an appointment with someone important, or a visit to an otherwise restricted area (the floor of a stock exchange, inside a military post, the dress rehearsal of a show, or the like).

Remember that special privileges are a wonderful source for starting word of mouth; people feel obligated to repay a favor, and talking about your products or services may be the easiest (and most effective) way to do so.

WORD OF MOUTH CAN BE CONTAGIOUS

INVITE CUSTOMERS TO TALK ABOUT OTHER MERCHANTS TO GENERATE TALK ABOUT YOUR BUSINESS

A little while ago, we designed a word of mouth program for a Southern California mortgage banking firm to remind old clients of its services and get them talking about other neighborhood merchants. We started with a survey to the clients of the banking firm, asking them to list any local retailer or service provider that has offered good help in the past. We tallied this information, amalgamated the comments, and created a small booklet. The booklet was available in the offices of the mortgage banker—given to everyone who came in to discuss a new loan or refinancing project—and it was distributed to real estate professionals and others in the area who might generate mortgage business for our client.

The program drew a number of favorable comments—by the merchants who were recommended in the little booklet and by the customers who used the referrals. Here are some pages from the booklet to give you an idea of what we did and how word of mouth, encouraged from Tower Mortgage clients, can then be passed along in written form.

April 1998

TOWER
MORTGAGE

Dear Friend:

This second edition of the Tower Community report has been completely updated. The first edition was published two years ago in response to requests for recommendations on various housing experts and home repair and maintenance specialists in the Cypress area.

The firms listed on the following pages have provided noteworthy service to us and/or your neighbors in the past. We think they may be helpful in meeting your needs as well. We look upon this list as a place to get you started in finding the craftsmen, contractors, consultants, and other specialists you might need.

Good luck and please call on us if you have additional suggestions for future editions of this booklet or if you need any further assistance in solving problems related to your property.

Gary R. Prince

OTHER KEY TELEPHONE NUMBERS	
Anaheim Union High School District	999-3511
Cultural Arts Center	229-6794
Cypress Chamber of Commerce	827-2430
Cypress College	826-2220
Cypress Elemetary School District	220-6900
Cypress Library	826-0350
Cypress Police (Non-Emergency)	229-6600
Cypress Recreation & Park District	229-6780
National Escrow	995-8644
NP Professional Services	220-9074
Pacific Bell	(800) 300-2355
Senior Citizens	229-6776
Southern California Edison	871-2100
Southern California Gas	(800) 427-2200
Southern California Water	527-2118
Tower Mortgage	828-0441
U.S. Post Office	828-2266

30

TABLE OF CONTENTS

3

ALL SECTORS

TINKER TOM

Tel: (714) 827-6038

Latches, screen doors, minor repairs, locks, toilets, faucets, fence repair. Residential and apartments.

TINKER TOM
6870 Via Kannela
Stanton, CA 90680

HANDYMAN

28

WISE LANDSCAPING

Tel: (714) 761-3044
Pager: (714) 346-8699

Residential and commercial. Full maintenance and landscape work. Major and minor tree trimming. For a sample of Wise's work, see Tower Mortgage's headquarters building in Cypress.

WISE LANDSCAPING
8681 Acacia Drive
Cypress, CA 90630

GARDENING

26

AN ALTERNATIVE TO DIRECT COMMUNICATION

GIVE YOUR CUSTOMERS AN INCENTIVE TO INCLUDE YOUR NAME IN THEIR COMMUNICATIONS.

Arrow 93.1, an FM radio station in Los Angeles, ran a contest recently with a significant monetary prize given away each day. Individuals were asked to answer their phone with a phrase that noted that Arrow 93.1 was their favorite radio station. It is a modern variant on the twenty-five-words-or- less essay contests that used to be an advertising favorite.

One of our relatives actually put the phrase into the message on her answering machine, saying: "Hi, you've reached Tori and Barry. We can't come to the phone right now, but please leave a message. And our favorite radio station is still Arrow 93.1."

What a terrific way to generate a simple word of mouth message! Friends and relatives surely had to ask the couple why the mention of a radio station, some details of the contest, about the type of programing on the station, about what they could win if they became regular listeners, and so forth.

Because most promoters do not think in terms of stimulating word of mouth comments, they could have made their idea even stronger had the station asked their listeners to add a personal phrase indicating *why* they liked the programing on the station.

Although not a program that every business can sustain—the Arrow 93.1 prize was $1,000 per day for a month—it is something a department store, large restaurant chain, major delivery service, or other substantial business locked in a tough competitive market can try as a way to get current customers to generate word of mouth for them.

GIVEAWAYS COUNT

START CONVERSATIONS BY GIVING SOMETHING USEFUL AWAY—AND LETTING IT SERVE AS A NON-VERBAL REMINDER OF AN IMPORTANT MESSAGE.

Some years ago, the Sheet Metal Workers' International Association, a major US labor union, celebrated its 100th Anniversary. One of the souvenirs chosen to commemorate the event was a metal perpetual calendar. The calendar was not only helpful—providing dates well into the twenty-first century—but it was meaningful in its reference to a major calendar anniversary as well as evocative of the metal working skills of the union's membership.

Our consulting firm had done a number of jobs for the Sheet Metal Workers' Washington headquarters. When we told some of the officials of the union that we were about to make a second business trip to Russia, they suggested giving the calendars to people as a gift. We happily agreed. In part as a result of this small gesture, the Sheet Metal Workers' International Association became involved in a project to bring innovative Russian pollution control technology to the United States. The technology could provide not only significant work for the union's membership, but also major benefits to the American people. The perpetual calendars helped introduce the Russians to the potential involvement of the Sheet Metal Workers' International Association, provided a lot of credibility to the American interest in the Russian technology, and later gave union officials recognition among Russian industrialists they met.

We suggest development of some special item as a way of evoking word of mouth about any organization, something that every employee or member of an organization could give away whenever an opportunity to stimulate future business presented itself.

The point of the special item is not necessarily to use it to start a conversation on the spot, but to let the item "speak" for the organization when the representative is not around. Properly chosen and properly presented, the item can remind someone of the "message"(whatever that might be) the next time the recipient is in need of the type of work done or service offered by the organization.

CONTESTS

CONTESTANTS LIKE TO TALK ABOUT THEIR PARTICIPATION, AND EVERYONE LIKES TO BE A WINNER.

ALL SECTORS

Contests serve the purpose of getting people involved with a product, service, or event and getting them to share their ideas with friends, relatives, and colleagues. The thought of winning *something* works so effectively that one mail order house conducts regular contests in which *every entrant* is eventually declared a winner. Contests designed to spark word of mouth comments are generally easy to enter, easy to win, and most of all easy to talk about. Take a radio station. It sponsored a "worst workday" contest among its listeners. Here were some of the entries from listeners:

• *One lady described how she set off a metal detector on the way into a courthouse. She unloaded everything—belts, ornaments on her high heels, bracelets, rings. Still the buzzer sounded. But how could she remove her push-up bra when she finally realized that the underwires were triggering the machine?*

• *A lady described her worst day as running into a police car on the way to the restaurant where she worked and then spilling coffee all over the traffic court judge who had stopped in.*

This type of contest need not be confined to radio and television stations, but could be organized on a periodic basis by retail stores, financial service companies, Internet providers, and the like. While receiving entries orally and broadcasting the subsequent results is convenient, entries can be submitted in writing and results included in an advertisement or a mailing to participants. To reinforce the word of mouth aspect of the contest, we recommend that the prize be something nice for the participant to have and something he or she can share with friends, relatives, or colleagues.

Contests, it should be noted, are different from random drawings. The latter relies on luck rather than skill to determine winners. The Turkey Store, a Midwest meatpacker, obviously hoping to encourage follow-on purchases, places a card in their packaging. Customers are invited to call a toll free number and enter a ten-digit number printed on the card. We did as instructed only to hear an imperial voice pronounce that we were not winners. No "thank you" for entering, no appreciation for using the product, no please try again. The process was deflating and disappointing. It made us think of the product in the same terms. That recorded voice could have identified every caller as a WINNER with some "winning" more than others—a big prize, a coupon for a future purchase, or a booklet of recipes at the very least.

DO SOMETHING DIFFERENTLY

GET THEIR ATTENTION FIRST IF YOU WANT TO GIVE THEM NEW INFORMATION.

The Frankfurt Book Fair has become the largest and most important trade show for anyone involved in publishing. There is so much to see in the week allotted to the fair that the organizers have invited souvenir vendors to set up stands along the walkways and outside the various pavilions as a convenience to visitors.

One of the vendors specializes in wood products. Last year he was offering miniature clothes pins. We saw them as unique paper clips, something to draw immediate attention to anything that might be sent to someone else. We bought several dozen as gifts for the people who help us with the activities of one of our subsidiary companies, International Publishers Alliance. We sent them the little pins clipped to the following card:

Dedicated to representing the titles and works of small and independent publishers at book fairs and trade shows around the world.

SOUVENIR OF THE FRANKFURT BOOK FAIR 1997

This miniature clothes pin, made from wood and perfect in every detail, is the kind of "paper clip" that is sure to draw attention to any document to which it is attached.

Godfrey Harris,
Executive Director

We saw the clothes pins as a terrific example of something our friends could use to start a word of mouth campaign they might be planning. Send these out and someone is sure to remark on them. If that kind of conversation leads to a question about where they came from—and that conversation eventually allows the giver to introduce his products or services to someone new—then it will have achieved a great deal for a tiny sum of money.

The lesson is not that miniature clothes pins have some magic, but that there are dozens of products that might serve a similar purpose in starting a conversation. Just keep your mind open and your imagination active wherever you might be or whatever you might be doing.

TURN TELEPHONE RAGE INTO A WORD OF MOUTH ADVANTAGE

PROVIDE A CODE WORD TIED TO A SPECIAL DISCOUNT FOR PEOPLE FORCED TO REMAIN ON HOLD.

The Wall St. Journal recently reported on something called "phone rage"—customers who are taking their business elsewhere after long waits on hold, no help from customer-service representatives, confusing multiple choice menus that don't seem to fit a need, and transfers that go nowhere. While the *Journal* quoted consultants recommending listening carefully, calling customers by name, and encouraging them to vent their anger, we have another idea that can work with any voice mail system.

> When a customer has to go on hold in your telephone system, have the recording apologize for the delay, but explain that in partial compensation for the annoyance of holding, all people coming to the store or using the facilities during the current month will be entitled to an *extra* 15-percent discount at the cash register or when ordering if they mention—or write on their purchase order—the BONUS WORD for the month. Use SUNOB (bonus spelled backwards) or anything else that is short, easy, and snappy.

What are the word of mouth benefits with a program like this? We think quite a few:

- A person on hold gets an immediate reward for spending what for that person might be negative time—fixing a problem of the business's making.

- The store or facility has surprised customers with something unusual that will reward them immediately and unexpectedly.

- Customers have suddenly been empowered with something of real value to someone else—the code word. If you came into this knowledge, don't you think you might share it with someone else so that that person might benefit from the *extra* discount?

- Can you think of an easier way to spark word of mouth comments and draw additional sales to your business while creating instant smiles and rapport between customer and employee as soon as the bonus word is uttered?

Finally, studies indicate that 85 percent of callers prefer to learn something from a business while on hold, rather than listen to music or a radio station. More significantly, 15 percent of the 85 percent buy something they heard about while on hold.

THE "INNOMAN" NEEDS TO BE INVENTED

A NEW WAY TO DEAL WITH INNOVATIVE IDEAS FROM CUSTOMERS AND EMPLOYEES.

Just as the ombudsman was invented as a way to bring some compassion and fairness to bureaucracies that had come to work by rules of their own making to suit needs of their own definition, so we believe the world needs to establish a new official in large corporations and government agencies to deal objectively with the ideas and suggestions coming from inside and outside the organization. We call this office the "Innoman."

In many organizations today, innovations are either submitted or routed to the unit most likely to be able to implement the new concept. A suggestion for a new procedure goes to operations, a new packaging design is sent to marketing, a new leave policy to personnel. While most people would expect these entities to review the innovation openly and fairly, all kinds of factors interfere with their objectivity. For one thing, change is disruptive of established routines in a large organization; any change—even obviously beneficial changes like buying word processors to replace typewriters—can cause mistakes, delays, stress, losses, and unforeseen problems.

As a result, the natural tendency in most bureaucracies is to resist new ideas as generally much more trouble than they are worth; if not rejected by sheer laziness, then bureaucracies tend to trash new ideas on the basis of the NIH (Not Invented Here) factor. If an outsider can suggest something innovative that ought to have been developed internally—after all it *is* part of the job— then the bureaucrats might be viewed as unnecessary or unfit for the work. Result? Treat new ideas as difficult problems rather than opportunities for improvement.

To solve the problem, we suggest creation of the Innoman—someone at the center of an organization responsible for looking objectively at all sugges- tions, ideas, and innovative solutions in any area of a company or government agency. This person would be charged with overcoming built- in bias, prejudice, conflict of interest, self-interest, and other bureaucratic deterrents to giving an idea a fresh look and fair analysis. In many cases, ideas and suggestions might have to be returned for revision or further development if they have obvious flaws, are contrary to law, or need more thought. In some cases, the staff of the Innoman might provide consulting services to help resolve questions or refine an idea to make it fit better with the organization's culture.

What has the Innoman to do with word of mouth? Plenty. How people think and talk about an organization or its products/services may be determined by customer surveys or focus groups, but a lot comes fresh and heartfelt in customer letters, faxes, EMail postings, and phone calls of praise or criticism. Like new ideas and suggestions, these communications are routed to the unit of an organization closest to the issue. If the unit is the cause of a negative impression, the customer is not likely to have a resolution of the problem for some of the same reasons pointed out above; if the customer is offering praise or appreciation, most units would prefer that their superiors read it first. In short, we see the Innoman as a major new way to build positive word of mouth programs for the organization or limit the damage of negative word of mouth comments.

ALL SECTORS

TEMPORARY TATTOOS

PROJECT YOUR WORD OF MOUTH MESSAGE IN AN ENTIRELY NEW WAY!

We received a card deck solicitation the other day inviting us to order 1000 small transfers with our company's logo imprinted on it. The transfers are intended for use as temporary tattoos, but they look enough like the real thing to fool a lot of people and spark a conversation about a new body decoration.

We gave the card about five seconds' consideration—longer than most of the cards in a deck, probably because of the pretty model used to show where the tattoo could be placed—before tossing it in the waste basket. But a little while later, we were fishing in the trash to retrieve the card for possible future use as a word of mouth engine. As we thought about it, we could see these tattoos worn by chic women as well as macho men wanting to have some fun. Wouldn't you be tempted to comment on a tattoo carrying some commercial, political, or social message—showing up on a shoulder or a bicep, at the wrist or on the hip? Wouldn't that be an easy way to start a conversation about something of importance to you?

Clearly, this isn't a program for every organization...but it might make a sparkling Christmas give-away for company officials to send to the family members of employees; it might be something a union could promote to draw non-union members into conversations; and it could be slipped into every invoice, every package mailed out, or every bag filled with a customer's purchases.

Here are the particulars on the company that sponsored the card deck entry.

LogoPromo
1295 Shaw Avenue—#130
Clovis, CA 93612-3931
(1) 209 323 4500

ASK FOR WHAT YOU WANT

THE EASIEST WORD OF MOUTH PROGRAM TO DEVELOP STARTS WITH A DIRECT REQUEST.

Asking for help is the most direct way to stimulate word of mouth comments between current customers and potential customers. Even if the target for the word of mouth comment isn't inclined to make a call, you will still have stimulated the target's mythical "help" glands to consider buying a product, whatever it is you are selling.

The "help" glands are located in a part of the conscience where people's desire to do a good deed or be liked or contribute something to someone else are lodged. If the customer can't buy, providing the kind of help that word of mouth entails can also dissipate whatever guilt a customer may experience.

Try it. Ask people to help you get business with a specific request to call someone about the products you have or the services you offer. See how willing they are to pitch in with a phone call and a little endorsement. If they do it, be sure to follow up and report back to the person who helped you with the results of their contact.

Remember the old saying: It is surprising what you get when you ask for what you want!

PUT THE THOUGHT IN FORTUNE COOKIES

CHINESE-AMERICANS MAY HAVE INVENTED THEM, BUT EVERYONE ELSE CAN BENEFIT FROM THE CONCEPT.

Most of us have had the fun of being offered a fortune cookie at the conclusion of a meal at a Chinese restaurant. The sayings vary from time to time and from bakery to bakery, but most convey a measure of hope for the future:

- *You will meet someone important to your success.*
- *Be prepared to spend extra money coming your way next year.*
- *Good health awaits you.*
- *A thrilling time is ahead for you.*

Recently, a number of companies have been offering novelty fortune cookies as gifts for special occasions. In these cases, the fortune is not a look at the future, but a message of good cheer or greeting—Happy Birthday, Enjoy Your Anniversary, and so forth.

It struck us that the same concept could be successfully used as a word of mouth device. Send a few of these to your clients at odd times of the year (Chinese New Year, the anniversary of the return of Hong Kong to Beijing's control, National Friendship Day) or when you want to acknowledge something that a customer has done for you.

If we sent out Fortune Cookies, our message might be a reminder of some of the basic principles underlying word of mouth advertising:

- *Word of Mouth Reminder: Acknowledge Everything!*
- *Word of Mouth Reminder: Ask for What You Want.*
- *Word of Mouth Reminder: Stay in Touch!*
- *Word of Mouth Reminder: Surprise Someone Today.*
- *Word of Mouth Reminder: Be Original in Everything You Do.*
- *Word of Mouth Reminder: Do Something Nice for Someone Else.*
- *Word of Mouth Reminder: Send Two of Everything!*

Of course, there are many other choices of themes for messages. They could convey something interesting about your products, services, or an upcoming event: "XYZ Improves Your Love Life" or "Enjoy ABC Now, Buy it Later, and Pay Whenever." By the same token, the message inside the fortune cookie need not be a message, but could be a discount coupon, voucher, or some other entitlement or combination of message and reward.

COMPENSATE NEGATIVE TIME

IF YOU ASK CUSTOMERS FOR A FAVOR, BE SURE TO REWARD THEM.

We have all been asked to spend time looking for a receipt, a cancelled check, a copy of a memo, or some other item that takes time, but offers no realistic hope of yielding any benefit to the individual doing the searching. The best that can be said for most of the negative time spent is that solving the problem may prevent some greater agony at some future point in time—responding to a law suit, cleaning up a credit record, getting a person or company to respond to your need in the future.

If you have to ask someone to look for something for you, fill out a questionnaire, return a product in a recall, or otherwise impose on their time, you can get people talking about your products or services by dropping them a note to let them know that you appreciated the time they took to resolve the matter and that you have done something for them in return—sent a donation to a charity in their name, bought them a lottery ticket, or found some gift that you hope they can use.

Why is saying you're sorry so hard for some people to do, when it is one of the least expensive, most important ways to generate positive word of mouth comments about your products, services, or event?

MAKE THEM FEEL GOOD!

GIVE CUSTOMERS SOMETHING TO GIVE TO THEIR CUSTOMERS—AND RECIPIENTS MAY COME TO USE YOUR SERVICES AS WELL.

We have some European friends who always come to our house with a bouquet of flowers and never go to the doctor's office for an appointment without little gifts for the physician and the nurses. While we protest that they shouldn't bring us anything, it never dissuades them—and it never fails to evoke a smile from us and a feeling of pleasure at seeing them again.

The concept sparked a similar idea for a small business we advise. We suggested to the owner that he have some stickers made with the following slogan imprinted:

> **DO**
> **SOMETHING**
> **THOUGHTFUL**
> **FOR**
> **SOMEONE**
> **ELSE**
> **TODAY**
>
> A pleasant thought from
> **American Microfilming**
> (818) 881 0072

Our hope was that after getting the stickers printed, he would mail a roll of twenty-five or so to each of his clients, urging them to put the stickers on their next communication to a friend, colleague, associate, or client. We said that the cover letter accompanying the stickers might also suggest what something "thoughtful" might actually be—compliment someone, say an extra special thank you for a favor done, send a gift or note in acknowledgement of a service, provide something (an article, a comment) the other person would appreciate, and so on.

We told our client that the idea is to get his clients feeling good about him and to realize that good guys deserve to be supported in *their* work. We call this the sympathy approach to marketing.

A MEANINGFUL
CUSTOMER NEWSLETTER

SHARE THE INSIDE INFORMATION ABOUT YOUR OWN INDUSTRY AS WELL AS DETAILS OF YOUR OWN COMPANY.

Most company newsletters sent to customers are either barely disguised advertising circulars for new products, upgrade specification charts, or employee-of-the-month bulletins. Generally, very little of substantive interest to *customers* can be found in them.

We believe that these journals can be used as a primary source for word of mouth promotion. We think the secret to achieving this desirable goal is putting the customer on the inside of what is going on in the industry of the company producing the newsletter. Most customers of a company never have a chance to read the trade papers and magazines affecting the company's industry. But it is exactly this kind of information, once shared with a customer, that can filter out to contacts of the customer and produce conversations that can lead to increased business for the newsletter producer—at almost no cost.

For example, if printers are reading about anticipated paper shortages in their journals—due to environmental limitations on tree cutting, excessive demand in various fields, or any one of a hundred other factors—they should add this information to their own customer newsletters. We believe in such situations customers would be more understanding of subsequent price increases and better prepared to conduct their own business as a result of the new information. Moreover, we also believe they would take pride in sharing the information.

Inside information is always hard for outsiders to get. But inside information in the information age is what gives companies and individuals an edge over their competitors. Customers regularly supplied with this kind of information are likely to show their appreciation—either through increased orders or in introducing the company's name to their own contacts.

If writing or producing something such as a customer newsletter is daunting—and no professional firms are available to take the burden from you—we suggest that you provide your customers with the news in the form of a letter. Write the letter as if you were explaining the industry's situation to a son or daughter away at college. Remember, the finished product is not a test of your English grammar or your writing style; it is intended merely as a powerful way to gain the trust of your clients and start word of mouth flowing.

HELP CUSTOMERS COMMUNICATE

INCLUDE POSTCARDS WITH GUARANTEE INFORMATION AND OPERATING INSTRUCTIONS FOR NEW PRODUCTS.

As we have noted, most word of mouth comments need to be stimulated. One of the oldest methods to accomplish this is the humble postcard—an inexpensive form of communication from one person to another. An enormous amount of basic information about a product can be pre-printed and illustrated, essentially to serve as conversation starters, with sufficient room left over for the sender to describe any personal impressions of the product before mailing. We suggest that manufacturers and others *pre-stamp* cards for inclusion in the packet of material containing the instruction manual and warranty information. There is something about a pre-stamped, pre-printed postcard that proves hard for people to resist using.

More importantly, most individuals acquiring a new machine, special accessory, versatile software, or particular peripheral spend a considerable amount of time studying the alternatives and options before deciding. But once they have made that final decision, they take great pride in becoming a new member of the team. (Do you know many people who trash a major purchase they have just made?)

The desire to share the knowledge and initial impressions gained is quite natural. Think how people like to show friends their new cars, the special features of a new television set, or the sound reproduction qualities of a new CD player. By the same token, many people are glad to have the benefit of the time someone else spent researching a new purchase. They would be happy to receive the basic information on a card and happier still to discuss the details if they are in the market for the same kind of acquisition. Given this cultural phenomenon, why not help it along with a postcard such as follows?

Thought you might like to know that we just had a nifty piece of pollution control equipment installed to give us the necessary capability to beat back NOx and SOx emissions.

The device is Russian-designed and uses high voltage electricity to split the polluting molecules apart. It not only works splendidly, it turns out to be relatively inexpensive.

If you are interested, I'd be happy to give you more details about the Pulsatech® device.

BASIC MANUFACTURING
PO BOX XXX
RURAL AREA, STATE ZIP
(800) 555-0100

PLACE STAMP HERE

UNDERSTATE YOUR STRENGTHS

LET CUSTOMERS DISCOVER ASPECTS OF YOUR PRODUCTS FOR THEMSELVES AND REAP THE BENEFITS OF THE CHAT IT WILL GENERATE.

It is a basic tenet of education to let students discover aspects of a principle or concept for themselves. I can still remember staring at a world map in elementary school while something else was going on and suddenly realizing that the hump of South America might fit into the hollow below the hump of Africa. It was a wonderous discovery for an 8-year-old and led, I think, to a lifelong interest in geographical relationships.

Despite the recognized power of discovery as a motivating force in human activity, it is seldom put to use by a major corporation in the sale of their products. There is an overwhelming temptation to extol *all* the benefits of a product to be sure not to miss any potential buyer's hot button. But we think using the principle of the power of discovery could make the next mega-success story for a business, such as American Express, Ford, McDonald's, or Microsoft have been in the past.

Here is the idea. Companies should consciously *undersell* what their new products will really do for a customer. They should allow customers to discover many of the applications, capabilities, and uses of the product for themselves.

Do you think that someone discovering something of value in a piece of machinery or in an information product might be excited? Do you think that person might want to share that excitement and knowledge with colleagues and friends? Do you think the excitement might set off an explosion of word of mouth advertising that might amaze even those who rely on traditional advertising? Do you think it might be worth it for a company with a good new product to try?

BUSINESS TOURS

BECAUSE KIDS TALK, ENCOURAGE TEACHERS TO BRING THEIR STUDENTS FOR A TOUR OF YOUR FACILITY.

Making the process of manufacturing something tangible or providing a complex service real to young students is a challenge. Moreover, teachers of older students always appreciate opportunities to show how work done in the classroom—math, verbal expression, history—can relate to work done on the job or in the marketplace.

While facility tours are certainly not new, targeting children and young people as the principal audience may be. Children are great vacuums—sucking up information as it comes to them to be reprocessed at other times in other contexts. They are also wonderful megaphones, capable of broadcasting what they hear and see to others. Think of the pre-teen kids you know. Don't they seem to talk incessantly about their activities with their peers as well as with their brothers and sisters, parents, grandparents, uncles, aunts, and cousins? Think of the teenagers you know. Aren't they always demanding reality in what they learn? Think of the adults who invariably assist teachers on field trips. Wouldn't they be impressed with what they see and learn on a shop tour, and wouldn't they be likely to talk about it?

Tours could be a regular monthly or quarterly event. Whenever they occur, they should be well thought through to provide information in an orderly and interesting manner. In cooperation with shop or site management, kids should be shown a process from start to finish, and every step of the process should be explained, diagrammed, or charted. To the extent that it is safe and possible to do so, kids should be invited to participate in some element of a job. After preplanning with the teacher, every effort should be made to relate steps in the process to something being learned or reviewed in school.

To reinforce the word of mouth purpose of the event, be sure to provide a souvenir of the visit at the conclusion of the tour—something that will be seen or could be used by third parties. It could be a toy hard hat like those given away at trade shows; it could be a sample of one of the products made or assembled in the shop; or it could be something as simple as a special brochure about the business with a pen, pencil, or other item personalized with the name of the sponsoring company. Each kid who receives a souvenir is bound to show it to someone else, and the ensuing talk may result in both new business and good will that will more than compensate for the cost of the program.

BASIC INDUSTRIES

One final point on the power of kids to communicate with each other in ways that adults will probably never fully understand and why businesses should see young people as important channels of word of mouth information. One of my sons and his wife have worked hard to filter the television exposure of their eldest son Kevin. When it came time for Kevin to graduate out of diapers, he announced that he wanted underwear with Power Ranger scenes on it. My daughter-in-law was stunned. He had never been exposed to their television programs, never seen the Power Ranger movie, and never played with a Power Ranger toy. But yet he knew that he wanted the underwear with the picture of the Power Rangers on it. A little investigation determined that a nursery school friend wore Power Rangers underwear. Kevin decided that to be as stylish as his friend, he had to have exactly the same thing.

When thinking about how to communicate a word of mouth message, don't forget the kids!

SEND A GIFT

PICK AN OBSCURE OBSERVANCE ON THE ANNUAL CALENDAR—FLAG DAY, ARBOR DAY, FRIENDSHIP DAY— AS THE DAY TO MARK WITH A CARD OR GIFT.

Once you have selected a day to commemorate each year, choose a small gift or unique greeting card that will remind your customers and clients of your business or product and tell them the reason that you are thinking about them on the particular day chosen.

Here is an example of a message that might be sent for Flag Day:

ABC Clothes
Street Address
City, State ZIP

Dear Customer:

As always, Flag Day heralds the good things that summer brings and reminds us that winter is only just around the corner. This June 14th we are again going to start manufacturing our range of wool shirts.

If you or any of your friends or relatives order before July 4th—for payment and delivery after Thanksgiving—we will give you our wholesale price. This amounts to a 57% discount from retail.

Sincerely,

Alex Benjamin Cox
Owner

Instead of sending just a greeting card, choose a special gift with your logo. Gifts given during the year, rather than at Christmas, stand out and are more appreciated.

If you adopt this word of mouth program, be consistent from year to year. While you may not generate a noticeable reaction the first time you use it, by the second or third year it will become a conversation topic among your customers and their clients.

This is a particularly good way for businesses other than those in basic industry—particularly those that pride themselves on originality and enjoy the humorous side of commerce (advertising agencies, artists, consultants, designers, entertainment or hospitality firms) to promote themselves through word of mouth.

ASK CUSTOMERS TO SEND MESSAGES ON YOUR BEHALF

ASKING SOMETIMES IS ALL IT TAKES TO GET A FAVOR.

We developed a Double Message Card mailer for a freight forwarding firm as a word of mouth program. The mailer consisted of a memo from the company to its customers and two identical, but separable, postcards. The memo reminded customers of the services provided by the firm and offered a discount on the next order placed in return for addressing and sending the two postcards to their friends, colleagues, and associates.

The entire package—printed horizontally on 8"x11" card stock—was perforated and scored to become a self-contained mailing piece. Here is a schematic model of how the mailer looked as it came from the printer:

The actual memo and a copy of one of the two identical postcards can be found on the facing page.

TO OUR CUSTOMERS:

We have delighted in providing you with
packing and shipping services
for the past 15 years. We have also appreciated the
consistent support we have received from our satisfied
clients.

As a way of saying thank you for your past
patronage, we want to give you a
15% discount
on your next shipment with us. (Just send
this notice in with your next shipment.)

Please also take a moment to send out the
attached discount postcards to those of your
friends and associates
who you think will appreciate the kind of
care and attention we give to every
packing and shipping task we are assigned.
Just fill in the person's name and sign the card before
addressing it.

If one of your colleagues decides to use
our services before the end of this year,
we will give you an
additional 10% discount on all
of your shipments.

Beverly Packing

Dear

We have recently been reminded of the fine service we have received from Beverly
Packing of Los Angeles. Our shipments have been tenderly handled, meticulously
packed, and promptly dispatched. We have come to believe that they move our
goods—from the point of collection to the point of delivery—more efficiently and more
carefully than if we were doing the job for ourselves.

If you have a chance to visit their shop on Fairfax at Melrose, you are sure to be
dazzled by the variety of goods they ship and the creative packing techniques they
employ to get valuable antiques, works of art, cartons of books, and oddly shaped gifts
to their various destinations around the world.

We think Beverly Packing deserves to be rewarded for the fine work they have done
over the past 15 years. In turn, they have told us that they will give a 15% discount on
the first shipment they do for anyone we recommend. This card is our way of referring
you to Mike Sarbakhsh at Beverly Packing. If you have any questions, please give
me a ring or please just call Mike.

Cordially,

PUBLISHERS [AND OTHERS] CAN PROVIDE TWO OF EVERYTHING

BUNDLE BOOKS, TAPES, GIFTS, AND OTHER MATERIAL IN PAIRS—ONE TO BE KEPT AND ONE TO GIVE AWAY.

We believe that publishers can start their own word of mouth about the material they produce with a simple device. Bind two copies of books, audio tapes, CD/Roms, and the like together with a pre-printed wrapper. We decided to use one of our other books as an example of a way to stimulate word of mouth comments. We bound two copies in a wrapper and reinforced the message with a sticker placed on the inside front cover of each book:

THE WRAPPER

> We hope you'll find
> *The Ultimate Black Book*
> so useful
> that you'll want to keep it for your own needs
> and so helpful
> that you'll want to give the extra copy to someone else.
>
> Godfrey Harris
> Harris/Ragan Management Group

We hope you—as well as anyone who receives a copy of this book as a gift from you—find it useful. It is our way of saying thank you for your support of our efforts on your behalf in the past, and we know it's your way of showing appreciation for your business associates.

HARRIS/RAGAN MANAGEMENT GROUP

THE STICKER

While the concept of selling two books or tapes for the price of one adds cost to a product, remember that the added volume being manufactured can reduce the unit price of each item to a manageable amount and can create impressive distribution figures that may make an important marketing statement in themselves.

The concept of providing duplicates of everything—one for an original user to enjoy and one to present to someone else—is a fundamental concept of effective word of mouth promotion.

HAPPY BIRTHDAY TO YOU!

DONATIONS IN LIEU OF GIFTS.

The Alzheimer's Association in Chicago sent me a blank birthday card at the beginning of 1998 with the the following wording:

> ## *Happy Birthday*
> ### *1998*
>
> _____   _____
>
> **With all Best Wishes
> to you and your family this year.**
>
> _____
>
> **In commemoration of your birthday
> I have given financial support to the
> Alzheimer's Association's
> Ronald & Nancy Reagan Research Institute.**

Nice idea. My wife's birthday was coming in a few days and I wasn't sure she would like the present I had purchased, so I wrote "Dear Barbara" at the top of the card, signed it in the space provided, and made a donation in her name to the Alzheimer's Association.

When I first saw the card, I wondered why no special envelope had been enclosed. Later, I figured out the reason. The donation form revealed that the birthday card was meant to be signed by donors and returned to the Alzheimer's Association for presentation to former President Reagan on the occasion of his birthday in February. Given my reaction to the solicitation, I thought the Alzheimer folks missed a better and broader variation on the idea—present birthday cards (and matching envelopes) that can be filled out and sent to those celebrating a birthday, along with donation cards to be sent back to the charity's Chicago headquarters.

It is a companion idea to the concept of hostess gifts found on p. 101. As we see it, people could pre-buy birthday cards on their own or acquire a package of, say, two birthday gifts and three hostess gifts. Bundling birthday and hostess gifts together into a combined package might make the idea more attractive to younger consumers faced with a string of upcoming parties and the need to find a suitable Christmas or birthday gift for their older relatives.

BE DIFFERENT WITHOUT BEING OUTRAGEOUS

IN POLITICS, BEING A LITTLE DIFFERENT CONVEYS INDEPENDENCE AND ORIGINALITY.

Doing something a little differently—an important axiom for anyone trying to develop word of mouth commentary—is doubly important for any political candidate. The "difference" should only be enough to cause people to pay attention; once a candidate has people paying attention, he or she can plant a party name or convey an idea.

We saw a political bumper sticker the other day that someone had hastily stuck on the bottom of a stop sign at a major intersection. It urged a vote on some long forgotten proposition that was identified only by its number: YES ON 205. We knew it was something debated a while ago, but we had no recollection of what 205 sought, when the election had been held, or how we might have voted on the issue.

But it did start us thinking that slapdash political sniping is a thing of the past. Putting up quartercards and stickers probably encourages more negative than positive votes, simply because people are tired of defaced public property and contributions to urban decay. That is when we thought that future political campaigns should create specific signs to fit in odd places or at eye-catching angles.

- Signs posted vertically, but with a horizontally printed message—something that takes a little head tilt to be read properly.

- Signs shaped to fit the space between the bottom of a brace and a supporting guy wire or even on the blank spaces of parking meter heads.

- Banners designed to wrap neatly around a telephone pole with the messsage spaced to be read from one angle only.

This kind of outdoor display is not, in itself, likely to cause conversations about a political candidate or issue; but it might make a sufficient dent on a person's consciousness to allow more substantive information to stick at a later time. In short, doing the commonplace differently is likely to pay dividends in the future.

RECOGNITION CAN PROVE TO BE WORTH ITS WEIGHT IN GOLD

GIVE PEOPLE SOMETHING—TO PUT ON THE WALL, WEAR, OR LEND TO OTHERS—AS A WAY OF REWARDING THEM.

For many years now we have collected archival material for the use of scholars working at the Hoover Institution on the Stanford University campus. The Hoover Institution is one of the premier research facilities in the world for the study of war, revolution, and peace. Because we have consulted on Panamanian/American issues for the past twenty-five years—and gather political ephemera, letters, photos, and other original material in the process—we have put together a fairly substantial file at the Hoover. Staff members, of course, are never satisfied. While always appreciative of our effort, they know that additional original material discussing the events and personalities involved in the Torrijos/Carter Treaty of 1977, the American invasion of Panama in 1989, and the events leading to the 1999 Canal turnover sits in garages, closets, drawers, and storage rooms all over Panama. How to get it?

We said we would like to help, but we needed an organized program to make our effort worthwhile. We suggested to William Ratliff, Curator of the Americas and International Collections for the Hoover Archives, that we co-author an article for publication in a Panamanian newspaper to explain the need and establish a reward for cooperation. We said that the article could serve as a "calling card" when dealing with individual Panamanians. We also suggested that something more than a simple letter would be needed to thank those giving material—perhaps a plaque, certificate, ribbon, or medal that recognized the contributor's generosity. We also thought that some kind of public ceremony in Panama, sponsored by the Hoover Archives, might be nice, and that a "surprise" award could also be given at that time—a special research card that entitled the recipient to use the archives himself or to invite other Panamanians to use them while visiting the Stanford campus. We argued that giving the giver something to give away would invest him or her with significant status and importance. We said that something of value and privilege in the world of academia is not something that often comes the way of people mostly involved in commerce.

We thought the chain effect might be infectious, and at almost no cost or risk to the Hoover Institution. We understand that the proposal is still being considered. Whatever happens at Stanford, we think it is an idea that any non-profit group should consider in its word of mouth programs.

EMPOWER PATRONS TO ACT FOR YOU
OUT-OF-THE-BLUE GIFTS ALWAYS EVOKE A CONVERSATION.

Many large charitable organizations have taken to sending an unsolicited gift as an incentive for recipients to make a contribution. Most of us have received packets of greeting cards or an oversized wall calendar in the mail from various organizations. Some favor scratch pads or refrigerator magnets; in the past few years, the gift *du jour* seems to be return address stickers in every design and format.

As we see it, these unbidden gifts are intended to play on some fundamental puritan value: Recipients will surely feel slightly guilty if they throw something potentially "useful" away, and they are likely to feel honor bound to "pay" for any item of value received.

It is not that we have a problem with this type of money raising program, it is that we think charitable organizations could do so much more for themselves if they applied a little word of mouth thinking to their incentive programs. For example, we suggested to the Stroke Association of Southern California that it send *two copies* of a particular reference book to those individuals who exceed a certain level of giving in a twelve-month period—one copy for the recipient to keep and the other for the recipient to give to a friend, relative, or associate.

We argued that when an organization sends a note of thanks for a donor's kindness along with a lasting token of appreciation, the individual will take the time to look at both items and decide how he or she will use the gift. But when two of the same non-consumable item arrives, the donor begins to think who among his or her contacts might appreciate having the extra copy. We believe that in nearly all cases the person who receives the extra copy out of the blue will call the donor to thank him or her for the gift. It is likely that the ensuing conversation will quickly turn to the original source of the gift and can, in turn, result in the recipient sending in a donation.

In short, many of our word of mouth programs are intended to achieve what a billiard player seeks from a richochet shot off of another ball. We want an added benefit from each thing we do by involving an organization's current patrons in an effort to get more patrons.

Because nearly everything involved with generated word of mouth requires a little push, we worded an explanatory letter for the Stroke Association to accompany the two research books we suggested they send. The draft letter appears on the following page.

Dear Ms. Supporter:

The Stroke Association of Southern California very much
appreciates your recent generous gift. We want you to
know that we will try to use this donation as wisely as
possible to assist stroke survivors and their caregivers,
to support promising research, and to join with other
health organizations in educating the public about all
aspects of this disease.

As a small token of our appreciation for your support,
please accept two copies of an intriguing little reference source. Why two copies? We hope you will put one in
your desk or briefcase, and we hope you will give the
other copy to a friend, colleague, or relative who you
think would also appreciate having this handy book. Our
hope, of course, is that the gift from you might spark a
conversation about how you obtained it and that that
conversation might lead, in turn, to increasing the
circle of support for our organization.

Of course, if you would like an extra copy or two to give
to more than one person, we will be happy to provide them
as long as our supply lasts. If for some reason you would
not feel comfortable in passing along the extra copy,
please do not hesitate in returning it to us. Above all
else, please know how grateful we are for your generosity.

                              Sincerely
                              [Signature]

NON-PROFITS

While it is hoped that every "extra" gift will result in a new supporter,
realistically we only anticipate a 10-percent response. At that, however,
the program has to be considered worthwhile.

COMMUNITY POSTCARDS

ONE CARD SHOULD BE AVAILABLE FOR FREE TO ALL VISITORS TO A PARTICULAR SECTOR.

A civic group, government agency, or community organization (a hospital, university, museum) should develop a postcard featuring an aerial photograph, reproduction of a logo, or other distinguishing symbol of an area. The cards should be given to visitors. What better way to start generating word of mouth about a particular place or facility than with a free card sent to the folks back home?

Businesses within the portrayed area would be asked to buy these cards from the non-profit sponsoring group with the message side of the postcard blank. Each participating business would be invited to submit a brief descriptive paragraph to link the business to the area depicted on the card. Messages printed on cards for different businesses might read:

- *Come see a museum totally devoted to pets at a 25 percent discount when this card is presented.*

- *All taxes and shipping free to anyone presenting this card at the time of purchase to All Boots Company.*

- *Enjoy free beverages with your meal when you show this card to your server.*

Once you have the cards imprinted with the facility's name, address, phone number, and easy to understand directions, leave them around a store, restaurant, tourist facility, or office, pre-stamped with sufficient postage for either domestic or foreign delivery. Be sure to ask your cashiers and receptionists to offer cards to customers and visitors as they are paying their bills or leaving a facility as a further way to stimulate their use and build future clientele.

To implement this idea, you will need a company specializing in printing full color postcards. For a current price list and sample, contact one of the largest:

US Press
1628A James P. Rodgers Drive
Valdosta, GA 31601 USA
(1) 912 247 4405

PUT YOUR TALENTS ON DISPLAY

SEEK A WAY TO HIGHLIGHT YOUR SKILLS THAT MAKES IT EASY FOR THE PUBLIC TO APPRECIATE THEM.

Members of the Sheet Metal Workers' International Association are expert in cutting and shaping metal. To emphasize the point, the union's seal consists of tin snips, a soldering iron, and a hammer. They are the skilled craftsmen who create the heating and air conditioning ducts in office buildings as well as shape the metal enclosures that shelter all manner of people and materials.

In thinking through what kind of word of mouth program might be appropriate for the 165,000 members of the union—to create greater awareness among the general public of the talents and skills of their membership—we thought of the idea of a contest among union members to design a special Christmas ornament—something to decorate the front door of a home or office or to be shown in a window, hung from a mantle, displayed on a table, or mounted on a tree. Part of the judging of the contest, as we saw it in our mind's eye, would be the elegance of the design itself and how well it conveyed the spirit of Christmas as well as the sheet metal arts; but we also hoped that the economics of reproducing the item in mass would be considered by the judging committee.

Our concept was for each member of the union to give two of the finished ornaments away to friends or contacts who are NOT part of the organized labor movement. We thought the gift would be greatly appreciated and we also thought that recipients will find a place for the ornament in their homes or at their places of work. If the ornament were packaged with a little message about the union and the origins of the design—along with an ever-so-gentle commercial that union workmanship means quality products and services—then we thought it could play an important part in starting a conversation about what union membership means and the value members of the general public can get from engaging union labor in their various projects.

We saw the project being an annual undertaking of the Sheet Metal Workers for the next several years, creating perhaps a set of five very collectable and very coveted items into the twenty-first century. And later, if the program proved useful in terms of expanded work and use of union labor, then the Sheet Metal Workers' International might consider sponsoring another Christmas project such as a tree topping ornament or special candleabra. On the other hand, the union might want to switch to another season and another contest: A weather vane that might be given away to non-union friends and contacts as a July 4 memento or tiny wind chimes that might be given to those who take little ones trick or treating on Halloween.

THE NON-PROFITS HOTLINE

CREATE AN 800, 888, OR 877 TOLL FREE NUMBER WITH A TIP A MONTH.

We think the telephone can be turned into an instrument of support for any non-profit organization in this way:

> Offer the public a toll free telephone service that provides important, reliable, and objective inside information about some issue—information that is not available to the general public and certainly not for free. The message might deal with any matter within the professional competence and overall interest of the non-profit group. We see the messages lasting up to three minutes, with a chance for the caller to leave a telephone number and window of free time so that someone local to the caller's location can return the call if required.

Reinforcement of the availability of objective, up-to-date information could be provided on the World Wide Web or as a Yellow-Page entry in major urban areas with a message such as:

> **HOT LINE**
> For free up-to-date hints and information, call the
> Non-Profit Charitable International Association.
> **(800) 500-0100**

To further support this program, we would recommend all members of the non-profit organization be armed with pads of Post-Its® to give to members of the public. The Post-Its®, including a backing card for a permanent record once all the sheets are used, might have the following pre-printed message:

> *Non-Profit Charitable International Association*
> Keep this handy pad by the phone. Call the number below for up-to-date innovations and information on matters of interest.
>
> **(800) 500-0100**

What are the word of mouth benefits from a program like this?

- A person gets an immediate reward in new "inside" information that costs nothing.

- Potential customers are empowered with something to share with someone else—*inside information*. If you came into new knowledge, don't you think you might share it with someone else?

NON-PROFITS

LISTEN TO THE PUBLIC

ASKING FOR COMMENTS STARTS WORD OF MOUTH OPERATING AND CAN CREATE NEW CUSTOMERS AT THE SAME TIME.

Many motorists, particularly in the larger cities, have found themselves riding on a freeway or stopped at a red light behind a car, van or pick-up truck sporting a red, white, and blue bumper sticker with the slogan:

UNION YES!

It's always nice to see this kind of pride shown so openly, but we have always thought that a bumper sticker can do so much more than identify the affiliations of the owner or driver.

Given the amount of training required to obtain membership in a union—and given the extensive certification programs that many unions offer their members to stay abreast of changing technology and legal requirements—we have always associated unions with *quality workmanship*. While it is true that some people automatically link union work with higher costs, others have shown a willingness to pay more for a job in return for better products and services. The Secretary-Treasurer of the Sheet Metal Workers' International Association put the point this way in a recent article in his union's journal:

> Would you [want] to...go to a first-year dental student or the best qualified dentist in town if a tooth needed fixing?

We would like to see union members change the nature of the public's general perception of unions with new signs that read:

FOR QUALITY WORK, CALL 800 UNIONS OK

or

ASK ME WHERE YOU CAN ALWAYS GET WHAT YOU PAY FOR!

The operators at the other end of the free telephone connection or union members themselves could be trained to make appropriate referrals to union shops in the caller's area.

We think this type of action-oriented message on bumper stickers, lapel badges, or hard hat decals could do a number of things:

- It would help more of the public associate the work of union members with quality workmanship.

- It would give people a place to find out more about union work and how they might hire union members for projects they need done.

- It would again offer a start on the road to word of mouth comments about unions and union workmanship.

GETTING THE CONVERSATION STARTED

POLITICAL WORD OF MOUTH REQUIRES A DOSE OF SELF-INTEREST TO WORK EFFECTIVELY.

As we have noted before, word of mouth comments on most subjects take some kind of push to get a conversation moving in an appropriate direction. By the same token, once a conversation gets under way, it has to move across a fertile field of mutual interest; people today generally have little patience and less time to talk about subjects that seem to have no direct bearing or little connection to their daily lives.

Political topics are a prime example of this point. Unless a personal connection can be established at the outset of a conversation, the subject will pass through the listener's mind with the speed of a bullet train. In such cases, the only impression left may be that the speaker is committed to one side or the other, but recalling *which* side that might be often proves difficult. Little information of importance tends to get passed on to build a meaningful chain of word of mouth comments.

As a result, we believe that political word of mouth commentary must emerge from a direct hit on an individual's personal interests, such as:

> *A NO vote on the transportation tax increase is a fake.*
> *If that issue is defeated, the politicians will use it as the*
> *basis for building toll roads to the new real estate project*
> *and do nothing about local traffic congestion.*

A message like that is something a listener can understand, accept on a visceral level, and easily pass along to others. In fact, when called on to make word of mouth work in a political campaign, we are always looking for ways to make the message personally meaningful and easy to articulate.

We also believe that political word of mouth commentary can come from an agreement to enhance an individual's personal power. In a world where people have come to feel helpless in the face of agendas dictated by big interests with big budgets, we favor developing procedures where ordinary people can feel influential long *after* an election has taken place. Here is one idea we presented to a candidate for city council a few years ago.

> We divided his electoral district into a grid, with each
> box of the grid containing some twenty-five to forty-five
> families. Starting with grids where we knew people, we

NON-PROFITS

designated one individual as a *personal contact.* We asked these people to suggest contacts in bordering grids. Each contact was then asked to be in touch with his or her their relatives and neighbors to tell them that once our candidate is elected, *anything* they might need from government should be requested through the contact and that it will be dealt with as if the request came from the mayor himself.

We told the candidate that during the campaign he would need to describe the procedure to make the concept come alive; he would have to identify the staff member—and the resources to be made available—so that his office could respond to the needs conveyed by the personal contacts. We argued that with a clear personal connection to the outcome of the election, all the people in the developing chain would talk with others on the outer reaches of their individual circles.

Expecting the candidate's other advisors to comment that the concept smacked of ward politics from the nineteenth century, we noted that it worked then and should work again. When others indicated that the idea had the ring of cronyism, we agreed again, but suggested that the circle of "cronies" would be considerably larger than is usually the case. When the candidate himself asked what would happen when there was a conflict between the requests of two or more different contacts, we responded that he would have to do what democratic politicians are paid to do everywhere—choose the policy that seems to offer the greatest good for the greatest number.

Eventually our client opted for an expensive conventional campaign of mailers, interviews, and personal appearances. Convinced that he could not win with a conventional campaign, we excused ourselves from further participation in the campaign. Whether we were right or wrong, the candidate lost to the incumbent by a large margin at an enormous cost.

THANK YOU FOR INVITING US

A DIFFERENT TYPE OF HOSTESS GIFT WITH TERRIFIC WORD OF MOUTH VALUES.

The other evening my wife and I had the neighbors for dinner, about fourteen in all. It was a nice event, but what stunned us was the value of the hostess gifts our guests brought with them. While a bottle of wine or a box of mints from a corner drugstore was good enough in the old days, people seem to be bringing much more elaborate and expensive items now. We received a large bottle of champagne, a giant tin of biscotti, a lovely ceramic stand-up picture frame with a bud vase at the back, a bottle of fine red wine with a personalized label, a proprietary specialty sweet from an exclusive shop in a resort town 100 miles to the North, a flowering orchid plant, and more.

As I thought the next morning about the generosity all of this represented, I began to wonder about the social tradition itself. Multiple single bottles of odd varieties, vintages, and estates may be interesting, but the sheer number suggests a wine tasting adventure that goes beyond either my wife's or my own curiosity. Worse, you can hardly serve everyone at a subsequent dinner party something different. Some would get insulted, others would feel slighted. Then I thought, who can stand the calories that comes in on this tide of sweets? Is it proper and moral to recycle these items as our gift to another hostess when we become the guests at the next function?

So a fresh idea with a word of mouth connection struck me for future hostess gifts. Why not something that goes on giving—a donation to a charity as an appreciation of an invitation to someone's home? As we thought about the task, we decided the logistics of the gift giving would have to be as easy as writing a check and packaged as elegantly as a fine piece of silver in order to work properly.

That definition gave us our idea. We think charitable organizations can create a hostess gift package to be pre-bought by individuals for a donation of a multiple of $50. In our mind's eye, the package would consist of a packet of five mock "checks" and five elegant gift boxes. Each "check" would have a value of say $10 for a $50 donation, or a $20 value for a $100 donation. Each "check" would actually be an elegant gold embossed form printed on carbonless paper. The original part of the "check" would be completed by the guest, designating the name of the hostess, and announcing that a donation in the hostess's name had been made to the charity in appreciation of the invitation to the function. The form would be placed in the box and given to the hostess on arrival. The bottom half of the "check," produced by the carbonless paper would actually be a self-mailing pre-addressed postcard to send to the charity's office so that the gift could be formally acknowledged.

We think this might be a very easy and meaningful way for guests to take care of their obligation to a hostess. We also see it as a terrific way to raise funds for a charity while also serving to introduce the charity's work to people who may not otherwise know about it. As a variation on the reverberation effect of the gift—first the gift presentation, then the subsequent acknowledgment—the charity might send a pin, magnet, decal, note pad, pen or other token for inclusion in each box with the "check." Other than the name or logo of the organization or the campaign, we suggest the simple phrase: WORTHY OF OUR SUPPORT! A message such as this not only automatically draws the hostess into the support group for the charity, but can evoke questions from others who see it to expand the charity's word of mouth reach in the aftermath of the function.

AN UNUSUAL IDENTIFICATION TAG

A LUGGAGE TAG WITH A MESSAGE CAN SPARK A CONVERSATION AT HOTELS, RESTAURANTS, AIRPORTS, TAXI STANDS, OR WHEREVER ELSE IT IS SEEN.

Here is a luggage tag we designed for a chiropractic office to save backs and spark conversation:

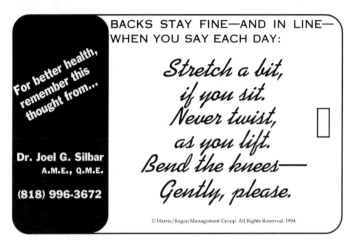

The identification tag consists of a pre-printed message on one side and a blank name/address card on the other. It is easily attached to briefcases, carryalls, backpacks, and suitcases with a plastic strap.

We wrote the above message for inclusion on a luggage tag when we were told by our client that many of the back injuries he treats occur when patients retrieve luggage from fast-moving baggage carousels, out of the trunks of cars, or off of the floor. The process usually occasions a simultaneous lifting and twisting or reaching motion—a very common way to pull a muscle or put the back out of alignment.

The office told us the tags were popular. We hope the message proved to be as well.

LET YOUR CURRENT CLIENTS AWARD SOME OF YOUR SERVICES TO <u>THEIR</u> CONTACTS

PUBLISH A MOCK PASSPORT QUALIFYING THE HOLDER FOR A VARIETY OF FREE PROFESSIONAL SERVICES.

Invite your current clients to take one or more miniature "passports" from your office. A professional serving in a law, accounting, engineering, architectural, design, consulting, delivery, or other firm should print the name of the client in the box at the top of the back cover (see top left portion of example below). Let the client fill in the name of a friend, colleague, or associate in the box at the bottom of the back cover before giving it to that individual.

A booklet such as portrayed here is easy for your local printer to lay out and reproduce for you. Ask him or her to provide blue card stock for the cover (reproduced on this page) and 20 pound white bond paper for the interior 4-page signature, trimmed to a $2 \frac{1}{8}$" x $2 \frac{3}{4}$" size, depicted on the following page.

P
R
O
F
E
S
S
I
O
N
A
L
S

[NAME OF CLIENT]

requests that the services described herein be provided to

[NAME OF CLIENT'S CONTACT]

[OUTSIDE BACK COVER]

Passport to Services from the Design Firm of

KLEVER, KAPABLE, & KAREFUL

[OUTSIDE FRONT COVER]

[DESCRIBE FIRM'S PRINCIPALS, SPECIALTIES, AND/OR HISTORY IN THIS SPACE.]

2

[INSIDE FRONT COVER]

[PROVIDE THE FIRM'S STREET ADDRESS, MAILING ADDRESS, LOCAL, FREE, AND INTERNATIONAL TELEPHONE NUMBERS, MOBILE PHONE/PAGER NUMBERS, FAX NUMBERS. EMAIL AND WEB SITE ADDRESSES HERE.]

7

[INSIDE BACK COVER]

The nature of the free services offered might differ among professional firms and craftspeople. Every professional can offer the services on the sample below—or might choose free paper shredding, excess office supplies, or even computer time as substitutes. Of course, some professionals may prefer to be more specific. For example, an appraiser's office might offer to calculate square footage at different locations; a physical therapy practice might provide exercise reviews; a jewelery store might provide free appraisal services; and a printing house might even offer to print business cards. Remember the purpose of the passport is to encourage a current client to give it to a potential new client.

When a recipient brings in the "passport" to send a fax or make a photocopy, someone in the firm would write the date and time the service was used and initial the notation in one of the appropriate boxes, just as a real passport is endorsed with an individualized date and port of entry stamp by an immigration official. It would also be useful for follow-on marketing if, when endorsing a "passport," someone noted the name, address, and telephone number of the holder and how he or she might have need of the firm's services in the future.

FREE TELEPHONE USE		FREE PARKING	
6			3

FIRST/LAST PAGE

FREE PHOTOCOPIES		FREE FAXES	
4			5

CENTER PAGE

NOT ALL WORD OF MOUTH COMMENTS NEED BE ORAL

ESTABLISH THE STANDARDS AND IDENTIFYING SYMBOLS FOR CERTAIN PROFESSIONAL ACTIVITIES.

The Good Housekeeping Seal of Approval long ago became synonymous with high quality household products. It was awarded to products only after extensive testing of the manufacturer's claims in the magazine's laboratories. Housewives knew that products carrying the Good Housekeeping seal were reliable, effective, and safe.

Other organizations learned from Good Housekeeping and created their own mechanisms for approving particular products or supporting particular technologies. The American Dental Association, for one, awards a Seal of Acceptance for toothpastes that meet certain minimum standards; the American Medical Women's Association endorses food supplements.

Any profession, whether formally licensed or regulated by a government agency or not, can create a system that allows the public to make instantaneous judgments about a professional's qualifications, experience level, and/or specialty. As a beginning, we would recommend that all professionals note on their stationery, brochures, and business cards the number of years in business. While not an audit-level endorsement, we think that longevity says a lot about the overall success of a business.

We also recommend that the firm's specialties be identified and, in some cases where appropriate, the principal clients they have served and/or the type of tasks they have done. We believe that this information, when recorded in an uncomplicated format, becomes an easy way for one person to talk with another about the qualifications of a firm and the services it provides.

If transmitting information about a product, service, business, or event is the essence of word of mouth commentary, then detailing basic information about a firm insures that the commentary will be effective.

DOCUMENT REVIEWS

PROFESSIONAL FIRMS SHOULD REGULARLY REVIEW THE WORK THEY HAVE DONE FOR CLIENTS.

Lawyers need to be in routine touch with their clients for whom they have prepared wills or estate plans; life insurance agents ought to be in communication with those for whom they have written property and casualty policies; safety and security firms need to talk to those who have acquired emergency equipment or plans from them.

Any of these firms should send reminder cards to their clients to re-read and revise the appropriate document. Use a double-sided card, inviting the client to check a box or sign a line indicating that the review has been completed. These cards can also solicit approval for the service—giving cause for word of mouth comments on the service—by asking whether the recipient wants a reminder in the following year.

MANAGEMENT AUDIT

It has been one year since we developed your Compensation Plan. Please review the documents in the Plan to determine whether any amendments or changes are now warranted.

Kareful, Akurat, & Barata Consulting

- - - - - - - - - - - - - - - - -

Date _____

We have reviewed our Compensation Plan dated: _____

☐ The documents are in order now, but would appreciate a reminder notice again next year.
☐ The documents need updating. Please call to schedule an appointment.

Name of Firm _____

CREATE CERTIFICATES YOUR CURRENT CLIENTS CAN AWARD TO <u>THEIR</u> CONTACTS

GIVING CLIENTS EASY WAYS TO PROMOTE YOUR SERVICES IS THE ESSENCE OF GOOD WORD OF MOUTH ADVERTISING.

Some years ago, we designed a word of mouth program for a research firm called MetroQuest that operated almost entirely over the Internet. The program consisted of three parts: An EMail message explaining the program; a certificate for the research firm's clients to award to a contact; and an action-forcing confirmation message from the contact back to the research firm that also served as a security measure.

Dear Client:

We hope that the research material recently provided proved helpful. Like many businesses everywhere, the favorable impressions we make on our clients serve as an important testimonial to our skills and responsibility.

We trust that whatever you think we did well—the scope of our research, the speed of our response, the reasonableness of our fees, the extent of our search, or some other service we provided—might merit a favorable recommendation to a colleague, customer, or contact. If so, we hope you will be good enough to award a Cyber Certificate in support of our efforts to continue to grow and improve our capabilities. The actual Certificate is on the way to you by mail; a replica is below.

Once you have decided who should receive this Certificate, please let us know the name of the individual receiving it on the accompanying MetroQuest Response Form (a copy of which is also below) so that we can respond promptly to their first search request.

In appreciation for your assistance and support with this program, we will be happy to give you a 10% discount from our standard pricing schedule for your continuing research needs within the next 12 months.

Mettro2uest

THE MESSAGE FROM METROQUEST

If you want word of mouth, put the words in the client's mouth.

PROFESSIONALS

METROQUEST
CYBER
CERTIFICATE

[METROQUEST INSERTS THE NAME OF ITS CLIENT HERE]

is pleased to commend MetroQuest's research services to

CLIENT ENTERS THE NAME OF THE CONTACT TO WHOM THIS
CERTIFICATE IS FORWARDED

who may request a free search for information or specific data within 12 months of

ENTER THE DATE THIS CERTIFICATE IS AWARDED

Please contact MetroQuest directly to initiate your search—a value of $75.

Certificate Number
1515-95 02 101

Internet MetroQuest@net.com
☎ (1) 212 555 0100
fx (1) 212 555 0100

MetroQuest Research Services
Address
City, State ZIP Code USA

PROFESSIONALS

METROQUEST
RESPONSE
FORM

To: MetroQuest   Date

CYBER CERTIFICATE

Cyber Certificate 1515-95 02 101 has been
awarded today to:

PLEASE ENTER NAME OF RECIPIENT

A LEAGUE OF THEIR OWN

CREATE AN ORGANIZATION OF RELATED, BUT NON-COMPETITIVE BUSINESSES, TO SHARE CUSTOMERS.

While many business people and professionals recommend specialists in their own *fields* for particular services—a dentist recommends an orthodontist; a dry cleaner recommends a suede specialist; an entertainment lawyer suggests a bankruptcy lawyer—few move outside of their own professional fields to recommend specialists in other professions.

We suggest working hard to create a league among service businesses—accountants, lawyers, financial advisors, engineers, architects, insurance agents, consultants—in a particular geographical area. Formalize the league by giving it a name, collecting dues, printing informational booklets about the members and their specialities, and providing a special free gift to new customers sent by other members. Establish common policies of services, hours, returns, discounts, sales, and more if the group desires.

We implement this concept at book shows we attend on behalf of one of our affiliates, International Publishers Alliance. When a visitor to our stand asks us a question outside of the interests of our participants—a recommendation for a specialty publisher, say, or a printer, distributor, agent, or other book trade specialist—we always hand them a card with our written recommendation to carry to another person at another stand at the show. The visitor likes it because he or she will arrive at the new place with credentials, and the company recommended is flattered that new potential business was sent its way.

Tower Mortgage took the concept in a different direction. They printed a little booklet themselves listing all the companies in their area that provide services to homeowners. See *Word of Mouth Can be Contagious*, p. 64.

CLIENT VOUCHERS

ALLOW YOUR CURRENT CLIENTS TO AWARD
DISCOUNTED OR SPECIAL SERVICES TO <u>THEIR</u> CONTACTS.

When a voucher for future services is awarded on behalf of its sponsoring organization by a third party, the voucher tends to have a greater impact and more perceived value than when awarded by the sponsoring firm itself. It also serves the same purpose as word of mouth without necessarily involving any conversation.

In this example of a client voucher, specialized technical skills are offered—as distinct from administrative services described on p. 104 or general professional services suggested on p. 108.

THE XYZ ENGINEERING COMPANY

- specialists in all levels of
environmental consulting services -
has asked its good client
to award this special voucher to

[ENTER NAME OF CLIENT FIRM]

[CLIENT ENTERS NAME OF ITS CONTACT]

entitling the holder to two complimentary hours of consulting time to evaluate any situation, problem, or matter that may require attention. Please call for an appointment.

XYZ ENGINEERING COMPANY
Street Address
City, State, ZIP
Telephone Number
Fax Number

INDIVIDUAL PRACTITIONERS NEED TO SET THEMSELVES APART

PICK AN ADVERTISING SPECIALTY, SLOGAN, OR THEME THAT CONVEYS WHO YOU ARE AND WHAT YOU DO.

Individual practitioners need to have something available that instantly identifies them and their special talents. In creating this item, individuals should be aware that it should help satisfied customers talk about the individual and new customers grasp their products or services. The film *Independence Day*, for example, is said to have done very well as soon as its insider nickname, ID4, was adopted by the public; Land Rover Discovery, perhaps hoping for the same kind of cachet, calls itself the XD. Communities are forever searching for the few words to frame themselves for their citizens, their neighbors, potential tourists, and industry. Bellflower, a suburb of Los Angeles, captures itself with the slogan: "51 Churches and No Jails." To rival the symbolism of the nickname, "Silicon Valley," the Greater Los Angeles-area has decided that it wants to be known as the "Digital Coast."

While we delight in conceiving these kinds of items for our clients to use to promote themselves through word of mouth, we know that generalizations do little good. A key chain is a key chain until it takes on shape, colors, illustrations, wording, and gadgetry that, together, serve as a clear reminder of the individual who presented it and the kind of work the individual does. But any apron, bag, book, button, cup, flag, tag, shirt, watch, or other item can serve the same purpose.

- A designer might create a symbolic logo that appears on a specially shaped mousepad to be given away to customers and for customers to give to their contacts as a perpetual reminder of the designer's particular talent, style, color sense, or artistic skill.

- A musician might record a CD with his or her signature style applied to popular hits to give to guests at a function to enjoy later and/or to give to others.

- An artist might do a sketch or watercolor of a scene and use that for calling cards, note pads, or greeting cards; a photographer might take the same concept—but use one or more images he or she has shot of famous scenes, persons, or events—to serve as an instant portfolio.

- An engineer might take something as mundane as a paper clip or as useful as a notepad and create something that would catch the eye and yet advertise that here is someone unique and worth talking to. Sometimes a note of explanation is required to link the item to the individual and make it easier for a recipient to pass along to someone else.

While the item is important in and of itself, distribution is even more significant. Before embarking on implementing this program idea, individual practitioners need to consider whether they will be comfortable writing a card or handing out samples or giving away unique creations at every opportunity that is likely to promote word of mouth. Failing a personal willingness to get the conversation started in this way, this word of mouth program may not be right for them.

One effective and convenient way for individual practitioners to use word of mouth advertising is to have a specially designed postcard printed for inclusion with every piece of mail—proposals, invoices, reports, articles, and so forth—sent to a client. We have them printed in two parts: A small perforated section on the left to carry either a pre-printed or handwritten explanation for the client, with the actual card to be sent by the client to a friend, relative, or contact on the right.

We recommend a full color picture that portrays the work output of the firm or the individual practitioner hard at work on the reverse.

| *Brief message to clients asking them to send the card to anyone who might appreciate your services. Remind clients to detach this note and encourage them to write a personal word to their friends and colleagues in the blank space on the card.* | Explanation of the individual's services with emphasis on what sets him or her apart from others in the same field. Offer a discount to anyone engaging the individual's services as a result of this postcard.
Name and Address
Phone and Fax Number

LEAVE THIS SPACE BLANK FOR PERSONAL MESSAGE FROM CLIENT TO ADDRESSEE. | |

BE SURE TO TELL YOUR FRIENDS

VETERINARIANS SHOULD DO MORE THAN
ASK PET OWNERS TO TALK ABOUT THE CARE RECEIVED.

A telemarketer participating on a word of mouth bulletin board on the Internet noted the importance of referrals—without apparently understanding the differenc e between referrals and word of mouth. He described how his veterinarian has posted pictures of the animals he has treated and their owners under a sign that reads: *"The Best Compliments Are Your Referrals."* The vet apparently reinforces the message by answering every thank you from satisfied patrons with a comment such as: "Be sure to tell your friends."

We think vets should go beyond asking for a referral to creating a true word of mouth program. Remember that referrals generally occur only when someone who needs something asks for a recommendation; word of mouth, on the other hand, happens when a happy customer does something that initiates a conversation with a potential customer.

As a result, we think vets might consider offering samples of a new commercial product—a food supplement, healthy treat, grooming device, or control mechanism, for example—one for clients to use with their own animal and one or two others to pass along to friends with the same type of pet. Vets could also offer special discount vouchers for friends of satisfied clients for such services as shots, examinations, and spaying and neutering.

In short, we believe it takes something tangible to give people a reason to talk about your products or services.

PROFESSIONALS

THANK YOU NOTES THAT CREATE WORD OF MOUTH

WHY NOT GIVE CLIENTS A CHANCE TO TELL OTHERS WHY THEY KEEP COMING BACK TO YOUR FIRM?

Some businesses have a pleasant ritual of sending thank you notes to customers at the conclusion of any given task. While they are nice to receive, we have often wondered whether they add anything to getting additional jobs from the same client—or new jobs from the client's contacts.

We believe that those business people who are inclined to send such cards are probably already recognized by the client as thoughtful, caring, and appreciative. Thank you cards probably add little to the impression. Instead, we suggest sending a cover letter with a voucher to the customer:

Date   **XYZ ASSOCIATES**
Main Street
Major City, State

Dear Mr. Prince:

We thoroughly enjoyed the time we spent on your project and delight in the fact that the end result turned out positively for you.

We have enclosed a certificate that you may be able to pass along to a colleague or contact. In appreciation for the work done and for your help in our growth, we will provide a 10% discount to the recipient and a 15% discount to you on all future work.

                           Sincerely,

                           X. Yale Zanville
                           President

PROFESSIONALS

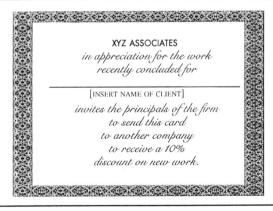

XYZ ASSOCIATES
*in appreciation for the work
recently concluded for*

———————————————
[INSERT NAME OF CLIENT]
*invites the principals of the firm
to send this card
to another company
to receive a 10%
discount on new work.*

REINFORCING WORD OF MOUTH

READ ABOUT THE MARKETING TECHNIQUES OF A <u>MOHEL</u>, A PROFESSIONAL ALMOST TOTALLY DEPENDENT ON WORD OF MOUTH ADVERTISING.

While word of mouth may be the *only* form of advertising for many businesses, most of these are illegal or immoral activities—drugs, prostitution, black market trading, spouse swapping, and the like. One above-board occupation that is also almost totally dependent on word of mouth advertising involves *mohels*—the Jewish spiritual leaders who are trained and licensed to perform ritual circumcisions.

Given the nature of the procedure and the fact that it generally occurs outside of a medical facility, it is clearly the kind of event that everyone wants performed with the utmost expertise. Given this requirement, no manner of media advertisement, no listing of credentials, no endorsements from well known personalities can substitute for one person's talking to someone they know and trust about the individual's skills.

We attended the *bris milah* (as the ritual circumcision is called) of a grandnephew a few months ago. What was so impressive was the way the *mohel* marketed himself throughout the ten-minute ceremony. He ordered the arrangement of the chairs and table as if he were directing a Broadway play; he explained the background and significance of every aspect of the ceremony with humor; and he used the back of a brochure that described his services to convey a prayer to be recited in unison by the people in attendance.

It was impressive. By using his selling brochure as part of the ceremony, he insured that everyone received a copy. By reiterating his explanations of the ceremony and the procedures he was performing with written descriptions in the brochure, he reinforced all aspects of his expertise, training, and skill for anyone who wanted to use or recommend his services later.

From every standpoint, it was a bravura use of a traditional advertising media to develop word of mouth comments. On the last page of his brochure, just below the translation of the prayer, were his telephone numbers, and, in the best marriage of ancient custom and modern technology, he also listed his web site address: www.torahview/bris.com.

SEND ENCLOSURE POSTCARDS WITH MAIL ORDER FULFILLMENTS

OFFER SOMETHING OF IMMEDIATE VALUE FOR OLD CUSTOMERS TO GIVE TO POTENTIAL CUSTOMERS.

This is a program designed for any business that sells products through the mail. Instead of loading a fulfilled order with yet another catalog, an envelope of coupons from other manufacturers, a surprise "gift, or a discount certificate for a follow-on order, why not try to build new customers through your old ones?

Here is the idea. In filling a customer's order, send along a pre-printed and pre-stamped postcard. Suggest that the customer send the card to a friend, relative, or associate. On the card, invite the recipient to send it back to the sponsoring mail order house for a gift that the customer thought the recipient would appreciate. Clearly, the gift has to be representative of the line of goods sold by the mail order house. Whatever it is, it ought to be the kind of gift that is universally useful and something that more than shows its retail value.

Once the card is returned by the recipient and the gift is on its way, mail a letter—and a similar reward—to the customer thanking him or her for the introduction. We think the dual gifts will result in a conversation between the customers and the gift recipient that will eventually prove advantageous to everyone involved.

Here is an example of how the enclosure postcard might read:

Just received some nifty items from Mail Order House. They included items you never seem to see in stores. Mail Order House asked me to send this card to a friend, relative, or associate who might also enjoy seeing something different. I thought of you. They tell me there is no obligation, no follow-up, no sale of your name and address, no pressure. They just want a chance to show you their latest catalog. Mail back this card in an envelope. They said they would also be sending you a gift along with the catalog to let you sample the quality of their goods. It sounds reasonable enough to me. **[SIGNATURE]**	Mail Order House PO Box XXX Rural Area, State ZIP (800) 555-0100 PLACE STAMP HERE _____ _____ _____ _____

PROVIDE TWO SAMPLES OF ALL NEW ITEMS

ALLOWING A CUSTOMER TO SHARE A NEW ITEM AUTOMATICALLY CREATES THE BASIS FOR CONVERSATION.

Grocery stores, restaurants, drug stores, and other retail establishments are continually bringing new products into their stores for customers to buy. But many customers tend to be reluctant to spend the money or give up on another favorite product to try a new item. It is a type of conservatism known to many companies.

Instead of asking customers to take a risk on a new item, we think that retailers (in partnership, perhaps, with manufacturers) should assume the risk for their customers. We suggest giving away generous samples of new items to introduce them. But instead of merely giving one sample to a customer, we suggest you provide *two* examples of any new item you want your customers to try. Whether it is a new recipe in a restaurant, a jar of mustard at a delicatessen, a natural cereal in a grocery store, some tropical fruit juice at a coffee house, a metal polish in a hardware store, or a hair spray in a drug store, package it in a way that lets the customer keep one example for him or herself and give a contact—friend, relative, colleague—the other.

Make sure you provide two copies of instructions or descriptions that give all the salient data about the product and how the item can best be enjoyed. Make sure, also, that the second package is convenient to present. Include *triple* sets of coupons with the samples for subsequent purchases of the product—one for the original customer to use, one for the recipient to use, and one for the recipient to pass on to a third party.

We think sharing the experience of a new product with a friend or associate will stimulate conversations and build word of mouth commentary.

RETAILERS

CUSTOMER APPRECIATION DAY

GIVE A BONUS DISCOUNT TO THOSE WHO BRING SOMEONE WITH THEM TO SPECIAL DAYS SET ASIDE FOR A STORE'S BEST CUSTOMERS.

We believe that retail stores might select a a day or two, no more often than twice a year, that feature special buys or special prices available *only* to the store's best customers and *their* contacts. Best customers might be defined as those who have recently spent more than $100, those who waited to have an order filled, those who have had a charge account in good standing for the past five years, or those who have some other distinguishing relationship to the business. To add to the appeal of these special Customer Appreciation Days, provide interesting souvenirs and exotic refreshments and be sure to engage a free valet parking service for the occasion to handle the crowd.

While sales are conducted for special customers by many firms, none that we know issues an invitation with an *extra* discount for those who bring along a contact to the sale.

We suggest mailing a card with the following wording to your customer:

> *Please bring this card with you to* **Customer Appreciation Day** *on May 15. Introduce a guest or guests to a manager, receptionist, or other of our officials on the floor, and we will be delighted to overstamp this card with a notation entitling you to a* **bonus** *10% above the 25% discount to which all invitees are entitled. Additional cards will then be issued to your guests to entitle them to receive both the special discount and this bonus discount.*

By providing an incentive for customers to invite and bring a guest to a special sale, the store is encouraging talk about its products and facilities *before* a purchase is made!

REWARD THE GOOD WORKS OF CUSTOMERS

OFFER SOMETHING SPECIAL FOR ANYONE IN THE COMMUNITY DOING HIS OR HER CIVIC DUTY.

Do you think people might talk about your business once they learned that you were offering something very special for anyone in the community who fulfilled a civic duty—voted in an election, attended a meeting of the City Council, served on a jury, fulfilled a military obligation, participated in a community's annual clean-up drive, provided a pint of blood, or gave special help at a local school, senior center, or other facility? We think word would pass quickly even if notice of the offer were just posted as a sign in the store or explained in a flyer attached to purchase receipts.

While these kinds of incentives have been sponsored by Chambers of Commerce in the past as a way to get out the vote for a local election—and caused a covey of lawyers to pontificate on whether such offers constitute vote buying or other illegal activities—we believe the concept should be adopted by individual retailers and broadened to any one of a number of important civic responsibilities. It should be noted that in the case of voting, many jurisdictions give a receipt, stub, or other evidence that the person has voted. If a retailer chose to select another civic event as the trigger point for his reward program, then clearly some form of evidence of participation would have to be established.

We would encourage any retailer interested in developing this kind of program to select a reward that really gives the appearance of something generous and special, and we would further encourage the retailer to provide the same reward to any guests or friends accompanying the awardee to the store to claim his or her prize. In the latter case, the guest learns about your facility and that good deeds are rewarded. As a result, the guest may become a regular customer, and the civic need may gain another supporter.

RETAILERS

MAKE YOUR COMPUTER YOUR INSTITUTIONAL MEMORY

BUILD A SPECIAL FILE FOR PROFILES OF YOUR CUSTOMERS' LIKES AND DISLIKES.

It has been our observation that most businesses do not gather useful information on their customers in any central place; rather they rely on statistical generalizations compiled by others or the institutional memory of an individual—the boss, a secretary, a security guard, a caretaker, a receptionist, or some relative in a family business—to remember important personalized details about their customers. Worse, few businesses see their customers on a daily or even weekly basis. While contact may be frequent and intense over a relatively short period of time—a lawyer preparing a client for testimony in court; a publisher working with a designer on a cover; a special occasion restaurant planning a birthday party; an architect designing an extension to a room; a restorer repairing a broken vase—most of the time months, and sometimes even years, may pass between visits of a customer to a business.

Yet nothing makes a stronger impression than being able to remember the details of past activity with a customer and being able to confirm vital information to make any new project move forward more expeditiously. As an example of what might be captured in a special data base on customers, here is what we think a restaurant might want to record beyond the obvious name, address, and telephone numbers (home and office) of a regular patron:

- Menu choices—appetizers, main courses, desserts, beverages—for both host and guests.
- Table preference—inside/outside, booth, window, smoking/non-smoking.
    + Server preference, if any—by name or by attitude (attentive? passive?).
    + Atmosphere—quiet privacy, spot visible to others.
    + Method of payment—cash, check, credit card (American Express, Diner's, Carte Blanche, Discover, Visa, MasterCard, dining club, other).
    + Celebratory dates—birthday, anniversary, holiday, special occasion (Secretary's Day, Valentine's Day, contract award).
    + Day and dates of previous visits in case a pattern can be discerned—Wednesday lunches, Friday dinners, first Monday of a month happy hours, and so on.

RETAILERS

Look how this kind of information, printed out for the restaurant's host to review before seating the customer on his or her next visit, might yield in the way of pleasure:

> "Nice to see you again, Mr. Thornton. May I ask Ella to bring you the usual iced tea? Wonderful. Mrs. Thornton: A Coke, no ice?

> "I recall how fond you are of our salads. Besides the Cobb you had the last time you were with us, we now have a new Mexican-style salad and a Caesar on the menu. I remember also that you remarked on our breads. If memory serves me, we even brought your party a couple of refill baskets. In any case, we have some new selections this month—a French roll and a Russian black bread—that I think you will enjoy. Let me know instantly if you need anything redone or refilled to make your meal more enjoyable."

If you were Mr. Thornton making a return visit to this restaurant after perhaps a six-month absence, would you be impressed? Do you think you or your guest might talk about the level of service and attention at this restaurant? We do. We also think this kind of attentiveness is the basis to get important word of mouth advertising started.

MAY WE CHECK YOUR BATTERY?

CREATE A REMINDER FOR YOUR CUSTOMERS AND A REASON FOR THEM TO SPEAK WITH THEIR CONTACTS.

Any shop or business that sells any size or type of battery—discount stores, office supply stores, drug stores, camera stores, computer stores, grocery stores, toy stores, electronic stores, convenience stores, gas stations, supermarkets, jewelers and the like—ought to send reminders to old customers to replace, recharge, check, or rotate the batteries purchased for their watches, clocks, radios, televisions, remote controls, games, flashlights, tools, fire alarms, cordless appliances, calculators, computers, mobile telephones, and other such equipment.

Any battery purchase at any store should trigger a request to the customer to complete a specially designed postcard. The card can be filled out in the store or at home—with the customer's mailing address on the reverse—and returned to the store for mailing a prescribed number of months later—depending on the average life expectancy of the battery the customer purchased.

Note that we suggest that the recipient of the card should take the opportunity of receiving the reminder to alert a friend or relative that they might want to check the batteries on *their* emergency equipment as well. With a discount offered to both individuals, you have stimulated word of mouth about your store and have the potential of creating a new customer in the process.

RETAILERS

Battery Reminder

If you wish a timely reminder to replace your recently purchased battery *before* it dies, please fill out the information below, address the reverse side, and return this card to the store.

TYPE OF BATTERY PURCHASED
[AAA, AA, A, B, C, D, N, OTHER]

NUMBER/DATE BATTERIES PURCHASED

INTENDED USE
[RADIO, TOY, FLASHLIGHT, ETC.]

The life of the batteries described above may reach their limit soon. Please remind a friend to check the batteries on any emergency equipment. You and your friend are invited to acquire replacement batteries at a 15% discount when you present this card at the time of purchase.

All Items General Store
1 Shopping Street
Anytown, State

EMPOWER YOUR CUSTOMERS TO REPRESENT YOU

DEPARTMENT STORE GIVES FREE GIFT CERTIFICATE WHEN PURCHASES EXCEED A SPECIFIED AMOUNT.

It certainly doesn't take a professional economist to figure that a $10 gift certificate given when a customer purchases $100 in merchandise amounts to the same thing as a 10 percent discount. But it does take someone who understands the potential of word of mouth advertising to see the advantage of offering the discount in this form.

Customers receiving the gift certificate can, of course, use it themselves for an item they might not have otherwise acquired. In that case, the store benefits by making an extra sale rather than seeing the customer "save" the amount of a cash discount in their personal bank account. But equally likely, the customer may give the certificate to someone else—a relative, friend, or associate—for that person to use. Whether the award serves as a holiday or birthday gift or whether it comes out of the blue, the recipient is drawn to the store, and some of the same advantages that come with more direct word of mouth techniques accrue to the store.

Any business should consider using this concept instead of routine discounts as a way to stimulate additional sales.

RETAILERS

DESCRIBE YOUR FAVORITE!

LET YOUR CUSTOMERS DESCRIBE THE BEST ASPECT OF YOUR STORE IN A POSTCARD, AND GET WORD OF MOUTH STARTED.

Proprietors and managers often overhear a person say: "I love this store!" or "I can always find what I need here." Memorable words to anyone in retail. But nice comments are like the sound of a tree falling in the forest; if no one hears the crash, what impact did the event actually have on others? By the same token, if someone who might benefit from the comments does not know of them, how can he or she benefit from the opinion of the customer?

Turning nice comments into more than a pleasant compliment is not difficult. Place pre-stamped, large format color postcards around your facility—in lounges, eating areas, waiting rooms, near cash registers, at customer service desks, and in racks at all exits. Post little signs near them with some nice elegant pens inviting people to send the cards free-of-charge to friends, relatives, or associates in town or elsewhere. To get customers to express their favorite aspect of the store, a message can provide the appropriate lead in:

> FGH Stores are famous for their motto: *"If we don't have it, we'll get it for you."* That may be true, but I happen to think that the very best thing about this store is...

We also like the idea of putting mock mail boxes near each area where the cards are distributed to give realism and immediacy to the program, as well as some privacy to the comments.

ASK FOR INFORMATION, NOT APPROVAL

ASK QUESTIONS THAT CAN YIELD IMPORTANT INFORMATION, NOT THOSE THAT MAY GIVE YOU WHAT YOU WANT TO HEAR.

Ever been in a restaurant when the server asks: "How's everyone doing?" It is the type of question that always seems to come when you are in the middle of either a mouthful of food or a crucial sentence in a sales pitch; at some Pacific Theatres in Los Angeles, staffers greet patrons exiting an auditorium with a friendly: "How did you like the movie?" Both questions invariably provoke a hurried "fine," "okay," or get an affirmative nod.

Most people don't want to interrupt their departures or the dinners they are paying for to have a long chat with a stranger about lowering the sound volume or changing a menu item. Even fewer want to have a negative conversation that something was boring or too salty. So nearly everyone that we know takes the easy way out; they duck the question by saying nothing of importance or agreeing on the excellence of the film or meal. But if a movie-goer or diner were actually masking what he or she really thought, that person may well express those thoughts to friends and relatives in what could become a negative fashion.

Instead of asking general questions designed to evoke a positive response, ask your staff to be more specific. Here are a series of questions that get information *restaurants* can use to improve their product without forcing their patrons to explain their views or sound negative:

- *Were all the vegetables hot enough tonight?*
- *Did you find the butter spread too spicy?*
- *Do you think you made the right choice for your main course this evening? If you had it to do over again, what would you have chosen?*
- *What can I tell the chef about how you found your meal tonight?*
- *If we could have done one thing differently for you this evening, what would it have been?*

We always recommend to our restaurant clients that if the person responding to specific questions has been articulate or particularly helpful in his comments, a manager should be summoned to award a special certificate for the person to use on his or her next visit to the restaurant. This not only dispels any negative feelings from the current meal, but if the certificate is designed to encourage the holder to bring along a friend or another couple, it can expand business as well. (See p. 45 for specifics.)

RETAILERS

PHONE CARDS FOR TRAVELERS

PRE-PAID PHONE CARDS CAN PROMOTE A BUSINESS AND PROVIDE AN INCENTIVE TO TALK AT THE SAME TIME.

The two phone cards pictured above were developed to give to people traveling to the United States from Great Britain. They were designed to reward travelers for choosing a certain airline or booking the trip through a particular travel agency.

But they also served as a terrific mechanism to encourage the holder to call home to discuss his or her travel while experiencing it. Nothing could be more effective in the field of word of mouth advertising than having people talk to others about a place or event in the middle of enjoying that place or event. The folks back home get news and impressions while they are absolutely fresh.

The telephone card helps the public convey those feelings in a way that few other word of mouth tools can. We think giving travelers $5 or $10 of free calling time on each card is a cheap price to pay for what may be a destination's most effective form of advertising.

WORD OF MOUTH CAN BE GENERATED—IF YOU ASK!

CHALLENGE POTENTIAL CUSTOMERS TO TALK TO OLDER CUSTOMERS ABOUT YOUR BUSINESS.

The realization that potential customers should be invited to speak to existing customers flashed into my mind while flying from Los Angeles to Boston: The leg room was some four inches more generous than on a competing airline's flight from Los Angeles to Salt Lake City—a trip I had taken the week previously. At first it didn't seem all that obvious, but when food was served I noticed how far the pull down table was from my stomach. I had to actually lean forward to take a bite, and I could actually slouch a little in the seat to watch the film without hitting my knees on the seat back in front.

What a pleasure, I thought. What a great idea for a word of mouth campaign as well. Instead of asking *existing* customers for a testimonial, reverse the process: Invite *potential* customers to ask someone else what they like about doing business with a particular company. "Have you flown Easy Air recently? Good, then tell me what you think they do best" or "Done any shopping recently in Big Store? How is their return policy?"

Challenge potential customers to go looking for friends, colleagues, and relatives—anyone who may have been involved with the company or a rival in the past. If yours is really a company or a product worth talking about—by virtue of its quality or originality—people will talk about it. Is this a big risk to challenge potential customers to find out for themselves about your company? Not if you are proud of the difference you make. Use traditional advertising, direct mail campaigns, or in-store programs to get people to find out more about you for themselves. In fact, use the full phrase on which the title of this book is based as the headline for the campaign: "Please, don't take our word for it, let our customers speak for us."

This idea also has merit for those companies with already established word of mouth programs. It takes some of the burden of *initiating* a conversation about a service, product, business, or event from current customers and transfers it to potential customers .

SERVICES

GET THE TALK STARTED EARLY!

SOME WORD OF MOUTH PROGRAMS CAN BEGIN <u>BEFORE</u> A PRODUCT OR SERVICE IS USED.

We have always maintained that getting the first customer is tougher than bringing in the second or third. In fact, if you can involve the first customer in attracting the second and the third, growth will be quicker and simpler.

Here is a program we developed for Amtrak's European marketing team. The idea was to provide two postcards for ticketed passengers to send to their neighbors. It was intended to not only provide worthwhile values to the passengers—leaving important information in an orderly fashion with people at home—but also to peak the interest of those receiving the cards to ask about the adventure when the US visitors returned.

Dear _____: _____

Date

We're off on a train-based holiday to America between _____ and _____

Our ticket allows us to stop when we like to spend time in the following places:

It should be great fun and quite a different way to see more of America. While we're away, though, would you be good enough to ...

❏ Collect the post   ❏ Water the plants   ❏ Feed the pets
❏ Start the car   ❏ Record Channel ___on_____(date)at __:__.

We would also appreciate it if you could look after the following for us:

In case of problems, we can be contacted through:

Look forward to chatting with you in detail about this rather exciting Amtrak holiday upon our return.

We adopted a similar word of mouth program for the Port of New York Authority. The Port wanted to encourage people using its airport, bus, and cruise ship facilities to spend an extra day or two within the New York/New Jersey area on their way to or from somewhere else. So we suggested a supply of double postcards be given to travel agents to distribute to any of their New York-bound clients. Like the Amtrak card, one-half provided information for friends and neighbors. What made this card different was that the top half gave the recipients some ideas of how to spend extra time in New York.

ENJOY A BITE OF THE BIG APPLE ON YOUR WAY TO EUROPE

Some "Don't Miss" things to do while in the city...

- an orientation bus tour through the canyons of New York
- a river cruise around the island of Manhattan
- a carriage ride through Central Park
- a walk through Rockefeller Plaza
- a view of Times Square at night

Some other suggested places to go and newer things to see in New York...

- The World Trade Center's Twin Towers
- Trump Tower
- Ellis Island
- Southport
- The Metropolitan Museum's New Gallery

GET THE TALK STARTED WHILE IT'S HOT!

POSTCARDS FOR TRANSPORTATION COMPANY MAGAZINES.

We have always believed that one of the best word of mouth promotions was lost when Howard Hughes hired MBAs to manage his Las Vegas hotel properties. In the 1950s and 1960s, every room was filled with postcards picturing and describing the hotel. They were free. It was hoped that hotel patrons would send them to friends back home, and, that those friends would later ask for more details and perhaps plan a holiday for themsevles. The professional gamblers that ran the hotels in the pre-Howard Hughes days instinctively knew the cards were a terrific form of promotion. But the MBAs figured that the same cards could be sold for a terrific profit in the gift shop. So they banned the free cards and killed a good word of mouth program in the process.

We think this idea should be adopted by every transportation company through their en-route magazines. We'd even take the Las Vegas idea one step further and recommend that the company offer to pay the postage for those cards left with company personnel at the end of a trip. Here is a sample we designed as a suggested program for AMTRAK's magazine.

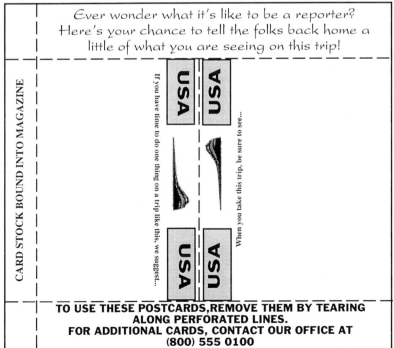

Ever wonder what it's like to be a reporter? Here's your chance to tell the folks back home a little of what you are seeing on this trip!

CARD STOCK BOUND INTO MAGAZINE

If you have time to do one thing on a trip like this, we suggest...

When you take this trip, be sure to see...

TO USE THESE POSTCARDS, REMOVE THEM BY TEARING ALONG PERFORATED LINES. FOR ADDITIONAL CARDS, CONTACT OUR OFFICE AT (800) 555 0100

SERVICES

LET 'EM STEAL

INSTEAD OF LOOKING FOR WAYS TO PROTECT THEIR HANGERS AND TOWELS, HOTELS SHOULD CREATE SOUVENIRS FOR PEOPLE TO TAKE.

Nearly everybody I talk to hates the hangers in hotel rooms that are attached to the cross bar. They long for the good old days when you could remove a sturdy wooden hanger, insert it into the shoulders of a coat or shirt, and re-hang it where you wanted it on the rack. Not today. Hotels, motels, restaurants, gyms, clubs, and other public facilities are so afraid that someone might walk off with an item that everything is either bolted down or designed for a single use.

We have an opposite view. We *want* people to steal handsome, interesting, or useful items from our clients. We know that if they do, the person will use it himself in his home or office or give it to someone else to use. Either way, we have a conversation piece for people to see, notice, and perhaps talk about. We think it is a terrific way to advertise.

Now, we understand the need to keep a room properly stocked with towels and hangers or a bathroom with toiletries and supplies. As a result, we recommend packaging a special item that bespeaks the place or facility, but does not deplete inventory for others. We have in mind a hotel offering a special heavy-duty hanger meant for hall closets—something the hotel guests could take with them, and something that guests in their home may see when they hang up their coats or retrieve them after a visit. The souvenir might be a hand-sized sports towel with the hotel logo that would be displayed whenever it was put to use back home.

As one famous management sage once noted, turning problems into opportunities is the secret to a successful organization.

SERVICES

HELP YOUR PATRONS COMMUNICATE WITH THEIR FRIENDS!

OFFER SPECIAL CARDS WITH DISCOUNTS.

Sometimes communicating with friends about the attributes of a place or the pleasures of an experience is not a simple undertaking. Restaurants, in particular, can make the task of communicating a lot easier by creating a miniature of their menus to mail to friends and contacts of their satisfied patrons.

We envision these minitaures as self-mailing fold-over cards. The front half of the outside cover would be used for the address and postage stamp, while the back half could be a photograph of the restaurant and/or a map indicating its location. Inside the fold-over, we suggest reproducing the entire menu or, if that proves impossible, displaying its principal aspects, highlights, or special dishes. At the bottom or along the side of the menu, place a message from the chef or owner inviting the recipient to enjoy a complimentary beverage when he or she comes in. Leave the pre-stamped cards on each table, along with pens and self-sticking seals, or provide a few cards, pens, and seals at the time the bill is presented.

This concept can also be adopted by other businesses, substituting samples of products and/or price lists of major services for the menu. Be sure to provide a message from management and a discount for new customers in this version. These cards can also be packed with each order filled.

MAKE PEOPLE FEEL GOOD

CHANGING THE MIRRORS. AND LIGHTING IN HOTELS, BARS, CLUBS, AND RESTAURANTS CAN CHANGE ATTITUDES AS WELL.

How was your trip? That famous question can usually generate variations of one of three answers: "Terrific," "Okay," or "Don't Ask." Did you like the restaurant? Another question that can evoke a variety of responses from "Wonderful!" to "All Right" to "Terrible."

While many factors go into an overall impression of a period away from home or a meal out, we have an easy way for many service businesses to generate good feelings about their facilities. We suggest that all hotels, restaurants, bars, clubs, spas, gyms, office buildings, and the like install mirrors with a very slight concave curviature and lights with a touch of an amber tint.

People using those mirrors under those lighting conditions generally appear thinner and healthier. It tends to give them an entirely new attitude toward their surroundings—they like being at a place because it clearly makes them look good and makes them feel better. We believe a program as simple as this will pay dividends in the conversations that subsequently ensue about a trip, meal, or place.

The relationship of looks to attitude was never better illustrated than when an executive of the famous Fedoskino box factory in Russia remembered a particularly tense meeting between President Carter and Secretary Brezhnev in the mid-1970s. The 200-year-old factory had been ordered to create a special box with Carter's portrait for a ceremonial presentation. Following the factory's rule that all the hand-painted pictures must be more beautiful than real life, one of the world class master craftsman had created a perfectly handsome miniature portrait of Mr. Carter. But the meeting was going so poorly that someone suggested that Carter didn't deserve the box. Nevertheless, when the box was eventually presented, the executive reported that there was a sudden shift in the atmosphere and that the subsequent discussions were much more productive for both sides.

John Roberts of Roberts Optical Company in Beverly Hills agrees that feeling good does have an impact on everything else a person tries to do, but he cautions against tricks in establishments where *merchandise* is sold. He feels people who come to him to buy a pair of glasses might be so disappointed when they see their purchase at home in normal mirrors and under plain lights that they might return the goods for a refund.

LET'S GO TO THE MOVIES

PROGRAM IDEAS THAT COULD WORK FOR THE FILM INDUSTRY AND MANY OTHER SERVICE BUSINESSES.

Most moviemakers need word of mouth about their films to help them survive in the marketplace, but as we have noted before, few do much about generating it. In fact, a startling number of misconceptions about word of mouth comes straight from the film industry. For example, a recent study by two marketing professors compared the impact of advertising and other promotional activities to reviews in drawing audiences to a film. Word of mouth among patrons was apparently not important enough to be considered. As a result, it was not surprising that the professors found promotional activities crucial when a film is *first* released and positive reviews important to helping films last beyond the eight-week mark. Wooing reviewers, they concluded, was like trying to "wine and dine the weather forecaster to get a really nice day."

A year ago we were asked to help develop a marketing strategy for a new film to be released by an alternative distributor. We noted in a preliminary memo that our programs were not a *substitute* for traditional advertising and promotional undertakings (interviews), but supportive of those efforts. As such, we hoped that the cost of the word of mouth programs we recommended might come from traditional advertising savings. "Rather than spend another $10,000 or $15,000 to make a two-page spread out of a full page ad," we argued, "might we get more real sales (rather than a greater impact) by using that...money for a word of mouth campaign?"

Here is a brief look at some of the word of mouth ideas we presented to the distributor to help promote a biographical film about James Dean:

- We called one of our word of mouth program ideas "Concentration." It involved posting a trivia question on a world wide web site as well as on a telephone answering machine hooked to a toll free number at a specific time each day. The trivia question would relate to something in the film—the color of a dress or tie, the make of car driven, what a character is looking at off screen in a particular scene, a word or phrase used to describe something, the relationship of one character to another, and so forth.

The idea of the trivia game was to reward individuals and couples in a fun way for seeing the film and getting them to talk about it in the hopes of finding an answer to the trivia question. We also thought it might encourage some avid fans to see the film more than once to have a better chance at answering the trivia questions. Individuals would be invited to call an 800 or 888 number or visit a web site to provide their answers. Individuals with correct answers would be placed in a pool, and a winner drawn at random. We suggested a prize of $130 per night (the number 130 was Dean's racing number painted on the car he was driving at the time of his fatal crash). Again, we had the idea of sending back the correct answer to the trivia question along with a discount ticket coupon for contest entrants to give to their friends.

• Create a very special and very valuable **newsletter** to take advantage of the fact that most famous personalities have a strong following in the general public. We saw the newsletter as providing behind the scenes information about how the film came to be made; facts about the number of performers, number of takes, hours devoted to editing—details, sidebars, charts, and photographs that go way beyond the normal information available to even the most avid moviegoer. We suggested that the newsletter feature non-published still photographs from the film, frameable photographic portraits of the film's stars in costume, notes on the release schedule, and so forth.

The idea behind the newsletter was to provide a foundation for how viewers should look at the film when they saw it, and most importantly, the phrases they could use in discussing it with friends. While we know that you can't put words in people's mouths, you can suggest the topics that create interest in a film. To do this, we had in mind having moviegoers assess if the film was "relevant," "detailed," "touching," or "exciting." We also developed the topics to spark after-film conversations: "If Dean were still living, what recent films would you have cast him in?" or "Being one of the world's most famous anti-establishment personalities of the twentieth century, what crusades do you think he would have been involved with had he lived—anti-war, animal rights, environmental pollution, anti-drugs, women's liberation, education." We suggested that the distributors offer passes to the film, as well as a coupon that could be used to have a portion of the ticket price rebated, in random copies of the newsletter. We also wanted the coupon to make individuals eligible for a drawing of James Dean merchandise. To make the newsletter effective as a vehicle for stimulating word of mouth, we offered a long string of suggested ways to distribute it in cities where the film would first be shown.

• As a third means of stimulating word of mouth commentary, we suggested the development of a **postage-paid postcard** that could be available in theatres showing the film. The card was designed to seek responses to three or four questions that were to be worded in such a way as to elicit the kind of comments about the film we hoped the audience would use to describe it to friends and associates. The card had two features: It could be mailed in, or the responses could be recorded on a toll free telephone number. All respondents would receive coupons to give to their friends to see the film and would be eligible for James Dean merchandise prizes.

We saw a number of additional advantages for the distributor in sponsoring this kind of an organized and coordinated word of mouth campaign. The mailing list that would be developed from the word of mouth campaign could be used to build public interest in future releases from the same distribution company. Further, the list could be shared with local exhibitors—whose cooperation and participation was crucial to the alternative strategy being pursued by the film distributor—in any special or future promotions the exhibitor might be asked to organize for a movie studio.

A final thought. We cautioned that programs aimed at stimulating word of mouth about a film could only be successful if the film itself had valuable features; bad films with few redeeming aspects would only provoke negative comments no matter how hard a distributor might try for a reverse effect. In addition, we said that if any word of mouth program were successful, its mechanics had to be kept a secret in the hope of using the same approach at a future time. The more people came to know about a program—or copy it—the less likely it would succeed in the future.

SERVICES

IT'S TIME FOR...

A TECHNIQUE TO REMIND CLIENTS OF THE NEED FOR A SPECIAL SERVICE AND ALERT OTHERS TO THAT SERVICE.

CLEAN YOUR PRINTER; CLARIFY YOUR IMAGE.

BACK UP YOUR DATA, LOSE NOTHING LATER.

Beyond the routine activities performed by professional firms are those specialized or exotic services that tend to differentiate them from their competitors. These services usually require only occasional attention, but may, in turn, be more profitable than routine activities.

Use a message on a calendar or wall clock or desk clock—like the two presented above—to remind the client of these special services. It will serve a modern service firm in the same way that Ben Franklin saved lots of people with his reminder to repair minor problems before they became a major catastrophe: "A stitch in time saves nine."

Trust the message to provoke a comment from any number of contacts of the client who see it. An office machine repair shop might use the clock face on the left, but a public relations firm could also make use of it. A computer consultant could distribute the clock face on the right, but so could any computer software or hardware company.

As with so many of the other ideas in this book, the message suggested for a clock face can just as easily be imprinted on personalized Post-It® messages to be given away to clients.

SERVICES

ANOTHER USE FOR POSTCARDS

CREATE SERVICE POSTCARDS FOR CUSTOMERS TO SEND TO THEIR CONTACTS.

While many businesses perform routine as well as specialized services for clients, others are only involved in tasks that are of an emergency nature. Take a roofer. While many homeowners would inevitably benefit from regular maintenance visits, most call only when they have a leak, find a shingle on the ground, need a gutter repaired, or discover some other problem.

The preprinted and stamped postcards, sent in an envelope by the roofer to his client list, are self-explanatory and designed to be sent by the customer to one or more of the customer's contacts, colleagues, or clients.

The postcard reminds customers to schedule a maintenance inspection to prevent future problems. We recommend that roofers—or any other service firm such as plumbers, locksmiths, security companies, glaziers, heating and air conditioning specialists, electricians, landscape gardeners, painters, drainage specialists, sand bag firms, and anyone else involved in emergency services—provide the maintenance inspections for *free* to start the formation of a word of mouth chain that can prove hard to break.

ROOF NOTES

Our roofer will provide us with our annual free inspection this month to make sure that everything is OK after the winter. He told me that he would be happy to do the same for my contacts if any of them wished to schedule an appointment with him. If you would like to take advantage of this very generous offer, please call Superb Roofing on (818) 368-4095 and tell Bill that you are a friend of mine.

Home/Business Owner

SERVICES

THIRD-PARTY WORD OF MOUTH

INVOLVING PEOPLE IN WORD OF MOUTH ACTIVITIES WHO ARE ACTING FOR OTHERS.

Many businesses today find that their potential customers are not going to be the *beneficiaries* of the services they provide. Take nursing homes. Often the investigation of suitable places for an aging relative to live when they are no longer capable of caring for themselves falls to a younger person. That younger person is going to make the decision or heavily influence it, and the younger person is going to be the megaphone for word of mouth comments.

Designing a suitable program for these types of businesses—funeral homes, specialized educational institutions, medical facilities, and the like—offers a different type of challenge. How can people who have no *direct* interest in a product or service be involved in generating word of mouth about it? We believe that the secret to solving this dilemma is making the individual thoroughly knowledgeable about all aspects of the business and/or industry to the point that they will want to share with others what they have learned.

We suggest that a company interested in generating help from third parties offer seminars to individuals on the company and/or industry or provide a special publication that appeals to people who advise others. While not a substitute for any other word of mouth program—many of which can be used to stimulate third parties into talking about the company—we do think it offers a useful supportive alternative in building word of mouth for those businesses that work with third parties who will talk to potential beneficiaries as well as to other third parties.

Another form of third party endorsement occurs when people recognize and remark on products shown in prominent use. Perhaps nothing along this line equaled the impression Sprint made with its name stenciled onto the headphones used by coaches in the 1998 Super Bowl. Name identification as well as a message of reliability in crucial situations were all conveyed to a huge audience for *free* during the action of the game. Some specialists believe that this subtle form of advertising far exceeded the impact achieved by any of the paid advertising spots during time-outs. In the same way, companies pay to have their products seen and used in high profile movies because of their value in generating subsequent conversation or emulation. The bottom line lesson for smaller companies is to look for ways to have their products or services used in prominent situations—for example, at charitable functions or televised events. It gives instant credibility and makes subsequent conversations easier.

DISTANCE DOESN'T ENHANCE WORD OF MOUTH

EVENT PLANNING GUIDE

Many businesses need a way to use word of mouth long after an event has passed, a product bought, or a service performed. Take a party planner. They help create a memorable event for a client that involves food, decorations, entertainment, venue, parking, and so on. Some months later, one of the guests at that party realizes that he has to plan a reception for his out-of-town clients coming to a convention in the city. The problem for a word of mouth specialist is to create a way for delayed reaction word of mouth to work.

We developed such a program for a caterer. We suggested that they offer an Event Planning Guide to their satisfied customers—something the customers could give to friends asking about who they used for catering services. We reasoned that something hard and permanent like a book would be kept on a shelf to become available when needed. We argued that most people do not organize their phone books or mailing lists in functional categories like the Yellow Pages—a list of various plumbers, jewelers, caterers, restaurants, airlines. Instead, people generally organize personal phone books and lists alphabetically and may not remember the name of a service company, even if they had taken a business card or copied down some information.

Here, then, is what one page of our Event Planning Guide, designed for Parties At Your Door, looked like:

PARTIES AT YOUR DOOR
21926 Costanso Street
Woodland Hills, CA 91364
TEL.: (818) 347-3044
FAX: (818) 347 7319

EVENT PROGRAM

EVENT TITLE

AT THIS TIME...	THIS ACTIVITY OCCURS...	UNDER THESE CONDITIONS...	AT THIS TIME...	THIS ACTIVITY OCCURS...	UNDER THESE CONDITIONS...

PHOTOCOPYING PERMITTED

FORM E

SERVICES

Instead of the Event Planning Guide, any firm requiring a long shelf life before word of mouth is likely to kick in may want to look at distributing a personal diary, a special calendar, a souvenir desk set, a mouse pad, and the like.

TALK RADIO
HOW TO SPREAD WORD OF MOUTH YOURSELF.

Nearly all the programs discussed have involved finding a way to get others to talk for you about the quality and value of the goods and services you sell. This program is a way for you to skip the necessity of finding message carriers and become the carrier yourself. It may not be workable in every community, but it certainly has potential in larger cities.

The concept is not complicated. Most radio stations create the programming they put on the air and sell advertising time to pay the costs involved. Some radio stations—as well as television channels—sell blocks of time to sponsors who create the programming content for the time period. On television, these are known as infomercials and often simulate the atmosphere and pace of popular interview programs. On radio, they usually take the form of call-in shows where listeners are invited to put questions to the host or hostess on the air. In rare cases, these paid-for programs are daily and may involve commentary and questions concerning the stock market, personal problems, or health matters. Weekly financial shows may deal with retirement plans or the relative merits of various investment units.

Subsidized talk radio allows a lawyer to field questions from the public about the quality of a potential case, a psychologist to offer advice on interpersonal relations, a travel agent to discuss aspects of cruising, a public policy consultant to talk about solutions to public problems. In between calls—like Russ Limbaugh, Don Imus, and others—the host can express his opinions, comment on events, or promote his business. In effect, the host becomes the vehicle for spreading word of mouth—mixing substantive information, helpful hints, updates on conditions, and advertising—about the products or services he sells.

Check it out in your area. It might work for you.

SERVICES

RESTAURANTS SHOULD GIVE "TASTERS" AND A GIFT CERTIFICATE

SINCE MANY PATRONS LEAVE WITH LEFTOVERS, OFFER SAMPLES OF SPECIAL DISHES TO SHARE WITH OTHERS.

Restaurants, caterers, delicatessens, gourmet shops, ice cream parlors, sandwich bars, coffee houses, tea rooms, bakeries, even health food stores and food markets should offer their special customers a sample of some specialty item to take home. It might be a particular appetizer, side dish, spread, dip, sauce, or dessert, and it might only be offered to those customers who order something extra such as wine, proprietary products, house specialties, or toppings. Whatever the item selected, it ought to have a long shelf life and require little or no fussing to serve. It should be packaged in sufficient quantity so that four can enjoy it. Print a self-stick label on a laser printer to identify the establishment providing the sample and give precise how-to-serve instructions as well as calorie, fat, and other content information. Present the item to patrons with their bills or as they leave an establishment—or offer the item to all customers at various holiday times each year.

For greater impact, we suggest that some food establishments present a gift certificate to customers along with the "taster." The gift certificate below is intended to be passed to a friend or colleague of the individual receiving the taster as an inducement to start a conversation about the restaurant.

[ESTABLISHMENT SHOULD PRINT NAME OF CUSTOMER HERE FROM CREDIT CARD VOUCHER OR SIGNED BILL]

is pleased to suggest that

PLEASE ENTER THE NAME OF PERSON TO WHOM THIS COUPON IS GIVEN

enjoy a meal and receive a 15% discount at

Name of Restaurant

Tel: ( ) __ ____
for reservations

Address and Directions to Restaurant

SERVICES

143

JUST BETWEEN US

SECRETS ARE A WONDERFUL WAY
TO KEEP WORD OF MOUTH FUELED.

In many families, some organizations, and various cultures, declarations that information about to be shared is a secret and should not be passed to anyone else is tantamount to broadcasting the news over the radio. Before long, everyone seems to become party to the "secret."

In a like vein, some years ago a company headquarterd in Switzerland set out to sell American mutual funds in Brazil. They became enormously successful when they discovered the power of the opening line of the sales pitch: "This is something the government doesn't want you to have." In fact, it was illegal for Brazilians to buy foreign securities at the time, but the very fact that it was forbidden fruit—and by something as hated and corrupt as the government—made the product all the more attractive.

It is a technique that can work well for many network marketers and multi-level marketing lines. The very fact that most of the products sold through networking are not routinely available from traditional outlets heightens people's interest in the goods or services—all of a sudden they are being exposed to something that makes them feel special—and, once sold they are more likely because of this feeling of specialness to tell others about their good fortune.

"Secrets" can be developed by any business for any product or service. They can involve special parking facilities, shopping hours, line defeating entrances, passwords for discounts or special treatment, or anything else that gives one person an advantage over those who are not party to the special information.

SERVICES

PAY ATTENTION TO WHAT'S UP FRONT

MAKE SURE THAT THOSE WHO DEAL DIRECTLY WITH THE CUSTOMERS KNOW YOUR BUSINESS AND WHAT THEY ARE DOING.

Word of mouth starts from good impressions derived from customers' having their expectations exceeded. Yet, those who are in closest contact with the public—particularly in the hospitality industry—are often the least able to communicate with them. The waiters, porters, maids, gardeners, drivers, guards, and repair personnel are seldom trained in the basic philosophy or procedures of the company they work for. Simple questions that should be answered quickly, only seem to confuse them. In some cases, language barriers prevent front line personnel from even knowing how to respond.

When you think about it, relatively few activities today put key personnel and decision makers on the front lines—pilots flying a plane, lawyers arguing a case in court, sergeants maneuvering a squad of soldiers against enemy fire, or doctors doing triage in an emergency medical situation. In most areas of human endeavor, the bosses and most knowledgeable people are somewhere in the rear, inaccessible to the general public.

When the lowest ranking, least experienced persons are on the front lines, customers can become hostile, and positive situations can rapidly become negative confrontations. By putting some of your best people up front—at a reception desk, in a trade show booth, on the telephones, even if only on a rotational basis for a day or two a month—not only can public perceptions of your operations be altered, but your best people can get a dose of the real world. Imagine what it would be like to get fast, thoughtful, and thoroughly competent responses to both trivial and difficult inquiries within moments of posing a matter to the first person asked.

It happens in Russia. There, receptionists personally guide individuals to the proper office. It happens in the Navy. A Chief Petty Officer at the gangway of a ship escorts visitors to their destination on the appropriate deck. It happens at some ski resorts where official hosts not only respond to questions, but willingly take a run with vacationers to show them various routes. This kind of up-front attention provokes feelings of warmth, comfort, and caring—something to convince even the most taciturn individual to be effusive about a place or business.

Sometimes, of course, it becomes a matter of basic economics—your best and brightest have to be put on higher priority activities away from public access. When this occurs, questions will still arise, and responses will still

SERVICES

have to be provided. We urge the problem be solved with a clearly divided, well-indexed manual containing the most commonly asked questions and the best answers to those questions. We recommend putting each question and its answer on a separate page of the manual, to allow for expansion and/or changes as required. These not only help less knowledgeable employees respond to customers, but also lets customers themselves solve their own needs if they are allowed to review the book

MAKE RESTITUTION FOR MISTAKES INSTANTLY

HAVE A CERTIFICATE OR COUPON AT THE READY WHENEVER A REFUND IS REQUIRED.

Nipping negative feelings before they can fester into a problem seems to be the best way to stop word of mouth comments that can turn damaging. Airline flight attendants issue cleaning vouchers; department stores issue refund checks. As a result, we urge all service businesses to have a certificate or coupon ready to give away for whatever need may arise. The certificates are designed to convert a negative feeling into a positive response or a positive response into an appreciated response by offering something that is intended to draw the recipient back to an establishment.

How often, for example, have you been to a restaurant, ordered your meal, and then found one or two items stone cold even though the rest of the meal is piping hot? Not hard to figure that something came in and out of the microwave oven with someone forgetting to set the controls. To compound this kind of problem, you can't ever seem to catch the eye of a server or a manager to point out the problem; sometimes, of course, you don't even want to complain for fear of inconveniencing others in your party. Later, when someone comes by to ask the inevitable, "How's everything?" the problem may be identified. But it's often too late to send the cold items back or to fix whatever else may have been wrong.

It's never too late, however, to try to make restitution. To do so, immediately offer a free dessert or a coupon for a free appetizer on the next visit to the restaurant.

Please accept a a free appetizer or dessert from

Good Food Restaurant

LET CUSTOMERS DISTRIBUTE YOUR PERKS

AIRLINES OUGHT TO MAKE FREQUENT FLYER PERKS A VALUABLE WORD OF MOUTH TOOL.

The number of places to earn airline frequent flyer miles has grown at a dizzying pace. Not only have regional and international airlines linked their plans to domestic programs, but hotel chains and rental car companies, as well as telephone companies and credit card firms, have joined with airlines to add miles to individual accounts. Other non-travel companies have created their own "frequent flyer" programs with look-alike clubs, memberships, and discounts to reward customers for their consistency.

The number of these programs and their longevity attests to their popularity with consumers. But, as far as we know, no one has yet used the frequent flyer concept as a word of mouth tool. We think airlines and other travel companies, long distance telephone carriers, and major restaurant chains might look at a gift certificate concept as a way to accomplish this.

> Instead of—or in addition to—bonus frequent flyer miles for selecting a given destination, traveling on a certain day, or booking during a specific calendar period, airlines might award the value of 1000-plus miles for their customers to give to a relative, friend, or colleague living in another city as an auto-matic discount on the next booking the relative, friend, or colleague makes. The amount of miles above the basic 1000 could also be rounded up to equal the distance between the customer's city and the contact's city.

We think a program of this nature would contribute further to customer loyalty, while creating new frequent flyers among the recipients of these special gifts.

LET IT BE KNOWN

SERVICE BUSINESSES SHOULD LET EVERYONE KNOW OF THEIR GOOD WORKS.

A janitorial company in California posts clear stickers on all the sinks, toilets, and other fixtures it cleans under contract for businesses and building owners.

We think any company proud of its maintenance and repair work ought to post similar information stickers in visible, but unobtrusive, places where they have worked.

The stickers serve as mini-billboards of a company's services. As such, they ordinarily wouldn't qualify as a form of word of mouth advertising. But precisely because they are attached to the physical examples of the company's work, they become a non-verbal means of communicating quality, while also serving as both a supplement and a spur to any comments a client might make.

SERVICES

WORD OF MOUTH PROGRAMS

LET US STUDY THAT FOR YOU

A WAY TO GET PEOPLE TO TALK ABOU TOPICS THAT DON'T USUALLY ARISE IN ORDINARY CONVERSATION.

Discussions about the company that provides your remote microfilming is not usually the stuff of ordinary conversation, even among casualty lawyers, claims specialists at insurance companies, or officials of government agencies. So to create a little word of mouth on behalf of one of our clients, American Microfilm Company, we suggested the firm offer to analyze a prospect's remote copying costs for free.

We knew that while many firms in the records copying field tend to ask for a similar per page copying and reproduction fee, there are wide variations in what they charge for multiple copies, mileage covered, time spent, process services, legal filings, minimum copies, delivery fees, and so on.

We felt that studying what a business pays for a particular service could give our client a double advantage: Our client could refine its own pricing policies to be more competitive, while at the same time offering the kind of free service that *does* generate conversation. In the end, the recipient of the study would learn more about his or her own business cost, and our client might generate new business as a result of the savings projected.

Even if our client did not land a new job from the study, it could generate the kind of conversation among similar companies that could result in new business. Any business trying to increase its market share at the expense of its competitors should consider offering to conduct free surveys and analyses for their prospects.

WHOLESALERS

SEND MYSTERY MESSAGES TO REACH NEW PROSPECTS

TEASING DEVICES CAN PROVOKE USEFUL CONVERSATION.

We have a new twist on an old concept—the tease. We have all been intrigued by billboards or newspaper stories promising that something significant will arrive on a given date—most often a new movie in theatres or a famous columnist in a local newspaper. The *Los Angeles Times* has been running a series of billboard teases that suggest that the full story can only be found in the newspaper. Here is the style: "Orange County has experienced a sudden increase in heart disease. Experts attribute the spike in illnesses to..." or "The 17-year-old manager chased away three graffiti taggers with nothing more than a stern warning and a ..."

Teases, if done well, get and hold people's attention until the secret behind the tease is revealed. Once a person's attention is engaged, beneficial conversation about the substance behind the tease cannot be far behind. The trick to launching that conversation is to make sure the interested individual samples whatever is teased.

We think new members of a network marketing line can achieve the same kind of result. But to make the program work immediately, they need a little initial help from upline executives. We recommended to one individual that he give all his downline people a supply of mailable pieces—postcards, greeting cards, letters—to pass along to *their* newest recruits for use.

The items we had in mind were pre-printed and stamped, with the messages teasing the eventual recipient's curiosity about the products. New recruits, of course, send the messages to their personal friends or business acquaintances, hoping to receive a note/call/fax responding to the tease. Each message could also offer the recipient a generous free sample—or it could be a coupon, discount, or other special advantage—as a way of encouraging the recipient to try the product (or service) that the sender is now selling or distributing.

The concept of a multi-level marketing tease is to inspire a call to begin a process where the recipient of a message eventually becomes a regular customer for the product or service and/or joins the sender's downline as a distributor.

WHOLESALERS

SURVEY YOUR CUSTOMERS CONSISTENTLY

REPORT THE RESULTS TO THE MEDIA.

There seems an insatiable interest in the media for the results of any survey on any subject. Do people really care about America's favorite fruit juice or whether dogs are more popular than cats? We suspect no one has dared to ask, but you can still see the results of surveys on the strangest subjects dignified nearly every day in *USA Today* and trumpeted as a factoid on CNN. While few people know what to do with such information as that more people suffer from heartburn than headaches (or vice versa), it is undeniably something to talk about.

We think the penchant for providing some kind of statistical framework for various subjects offers an important word of mouth opportunity. We recommend that you survey your customers on a regular basis on whatever your business deals with. Ask questions that yield responses that reflect preferences and offer some insight into future actions. Tally the returns, categorizing the respondents by location, age, gender, economic status, or other factors. Then look at the data accumulated and decide what is the most important finding of the survey. If this is a repeat survey from previous years, compare the new finding to others from the past.

Now send out a press release to every newspaper and media source in your local yellow pages and post it on bulletin boards in every Internet site that seems relevant. Send a copy of the release to your customers with a note of thanks for their participation. We think three things may well happen:

1. You will gain some information about the likes and dislikes of your customers to assist you in your business.

2. You will receive calls from the media asking you for additional details or further background on the data.

3. You will become better known in your field and therefore attract new customers interested in dealing with one of the experts in the area.

ENCOURAGE END-USERS TO TALK DIRECTLY TO YOU

WHOLESALERS NEED TO FIND WAYS TO MAKE IT EASY FOR CUSTOMERS TO TALK ABOUT THEIR PRODUCTS.

We recently shared a thought on the paper bags used by a local specialty bakery. The bread is terrific, we said, but the bags are terrible—too small. The manager of operations for La Brea Bakery called back, appreciative of the letter, to give us a personal explanation of the technical problems they were having in designing new bags.

After the conversation, we thought that while we are always motivated to suggest ideas to others—on the theory that one idea might get us hired to provide others—most individuals are not. They either have no energy to write a letter, no time to pick up a phone, no confidence that someone might care about their thoughts, or no incentive to offer ideas. If people have such little energy to offer their opinions, what would make anyone think that they would talk willingly about a product, service, or event— provide word of mouth—without some form of reward or incentive?

Businesses that are removed from the end-user of their products—such as wholesalers, distributors, and suppliers—should take note here. The bakery with the terrific bread is an example. It sells its products through supermarkets, delicatessens, specialty stores, bakeries, and the like. Unless a consumer calls them—and most that bother, do so with complaints rather than compliments—they have little idea of what the end-user feels about the product. While total sales of a product are the traditional capitalist gauge of success, the numbers often do not tell the whole story.

Here is how we suggested that the bakery might get end-users to communicate their thoughts about its products.

- Put a notice in with the product inviting the end-user to call and offering free coupons for new products if they do so.
- Put a survey form in with the product rewarding the individuals with free coupons if they respond.
- Post a notice where the product is sold inviting consumers to comment on the product or encourage them to offer ideas on new products that might be made.
- Print a message on the bag encouraging consumers to talk about their likes and dislikes about the product on the phone or via the Internet.

Once an individual articulates a concept and receives some feedback, he is much more likely to repeat it to others. The feedback tells the individual

WHOLESALERS

that the idea has validity, perhaps some importance, and may well be used by the recipient. All of a sudden, the individual feels important, takes a proprietary interest in the success of the product in which he has invested his time, and is much more likely to talk about his experience and the product to friends.

For the record, the bakery thanked me for the idea on the bags and sent me a generous coupon as a way of appreciation. It was very kind. By way of thanking them for their generosity, I sent a copy of one of our books and suggested that the next time they reward a customer they might consider sending along an extra coupon for the customer to pass along to someone else...and create even more buzz on a product.

OFFER A SEMINAR

SEMINARS TRAIN YOUR CUSTOMERS WHILE PROVIDING A FERTILE GROUND TO BEGIN WORD OF MOUTH.

We recently attended an Adobe Pagemaker seminar. It was designed to train users in the new features and benefits of the 6.5 release of the popular page layout software. We learned a lot from the presentation. But we also realized how effective these types of seminars can be in promoting word of mouth about a product or service.

Let us take you through the process we experienced. We received a card in the mail inviting us to the seminar on a given day. We could choose a morning or afternoon session; each session lasted two hours in an historic setting that was interesting by itself. The sponsors laid out breakfast for the morning folks and lunch for the afternoon crowd—all complimentary. The presentation was specifically pointed toward giving the audience some shortcuts to make their work easier and a full explanation of how (and why) the 6.5 version differed from its predecessor. To gain feedback from the audience, each attendee was asked to complete an evaluation form at the end of the seminar. As an incentive to complete this task, Adobe randomly selected various evaluation forms and awarded the individuals who prepared them a quality door prize.

The whole experience was so remarkable that I wrote a letter explaining that my "evaluation form...had not done justice to my feelings about the event. I...found the layout of the venue very pleasing and comfortable, the provision of snacks and drinks an act of generosity, and the attending staff most helpful in answering questions and managing the time available." In fact, I talked so much about the seminar—to EMail correspondents as well as office colleagues—that I realized that seminars, if properly done, offer a terrific platform for generating word of mouth comments about a product or service.

Think about it. When you train customers in your way of doing business—not only explaining procedures, but providing a rationale for your particular approach—you have not only made your own life easier, but you have added measureably to the efficiency and knowledge of your customers. Do you think they might share their newly gained information with others? Do you think that that might bring new customers? If our experience at the Adobe Pagemaker seminar is any guide, you bet!

WHOLESALERS

THE ULTIMATE WORD OF MOUTH PROGRAM
USE THIS PROGRAM WHEN
NOTHING ELSE SEEMS TO FIT YOUR NEED

Ask customers three or four weeks after they have acquired your product or engaged your services to let you know what they consider to be its greatest benefit to them. What are they getting from its use? How has it changed their operations? What feature has made the biggest impression?

These are not the kinds of questions usually asked on a warranty card (where did you acquire our product, how old are you, how did you hear about us, etc.). These are practical questions about how a customer has actually put your product or service to work for them. They are questions that are not easy to answer and sometimes the proper response is difficult to articulate. If your customers have any problem in coming up with an answer, suggest that they respond exactly as if their wives, their associates, or even a newspaper reporter asked them point blank why they bought your product or utilized your services.

Once you have the response—either verbally or in a written communication—send your customer an impressive gift that has nothing to do with your business. It could be a lovely clock for the office, a large box of cookies for the staff, a holiday flag to fly from the home. Make it unusual and thoughtful. Send it along with a note saying how pleased you were to have learned that your product or service has proven so useful or that you now know how to do better in the future to avoid the problems expressed. Ask the customer if they would mind if you referred future potential customers to them to talk about what you do and how you do it, as well as to discuss the benefits your products or services provide.

Most business people will be pleased with the gift and flattered to have such an easy way to reciprocate. From your standpoint you have acquired a spokesperson that already knows what he or she will say and how he or she will say it when asked.

Why, then, is this the *ultimate* word of mouth program? Because you don't wait for anyone else to initiate a word of mouth discussion, *you* initiate it. Moreover, by providing the listener for the person who can talk about your products and services, you have created the basis for a meaningful conversation. The fact that the listener is a potential customer, you have laid the groundwork for increasing your future business. If a word of mouth program can achieve all these ends, then you will realize its power and benefit from its rewards.

PART THREE

TECHNIQUES OF WORD OF MOUTH ADVERTISING

THE BEST WAYS TO PROVOKE
WORD OF MOUTH COMMENTS

Give the customer a push of some kind.

The best way to provoke a word of mouth comment is to *ask* someone, point blank, to tell another person what he or she liked about your products, services, or event. While most people in most instances readily agree to do so, they generally have a hard time discharging the favor—they never seem to find the right opening, right moment, right words, or right person to tell. As a result, surpisingly few word of mouth comments actually emerge from direct requests.

Because of this, we recommend that enterprises use a variety of techniques to make the process of talking about a product, service, business, or event easier for people:

- *Provide a giveaway*—Find something that others can give away on your behalf to start a conversation about your product, service, or event—a sample, a free gift, a coupon, a discount certificate, and so forth.

- *Provide a script*—Surprisingly, most people have difficulty describing aspects of a product, service, or event to another person. We recommend that you help put words in their mouths through a letter, postcard, EMail, note, or other device that describes what you do better than others and what specialties you are proudest of offering.

- *Provide information*—Information may be as valuable in the twenty-first century as gold was in the 16th Century. Information is the key to successful commerce. Give your customers information that they can't get anywhere else, and it is very likely that they will want to share it—and the source—with their friends, associates, and contacts.

- *Provide a forum*—Word of mouth can start when old customers have a forum to voice their views about a product, service or event. The forum could be a newsletter, a workshop, a focus group, a questionnaire, or a survey. The point is that attentive business people can use whatever forum is created to hear both negative and positive impressions.

- *Provide a surprise*—If you dazzle someone—amaze them, startle them, impress them—they generally want to share the fact with someone else. It is one of the best ways to get word of mouth started, no matter whether you surprise them with something to see, to use, or to experience.

- *Provide something of value*—There is an old saying in advertising:

  IF YOU MAKE 'EM LAUGH, CRY, OR SIGH, MAYBE THEN THEY'LL BUY.

  In short, most of us assume that people acquire products or services because they need them. In fact, most top flight sales people have long recognized that people buy things to gain a measure of pleasure. As one advertising specialist has noted: "People don't like advertising. So you give them things that delight them, that reward them for watching a commercial...." It works for word of mouth as much as it works for other traditional marketing techniques.

- *Provide repetition*—Have you noticed how often an advertisement you have seen a dozen times on television has failed to make even a dent on the consciousness of others? Advertisers know the importance of repetition; so, too, with word of mouth. As a general rule, we advise clients to repeat their programs, their ideas, and their requests with their customers until they begin to work. Once they have demonstrated some response, additions or changes can be contemplated to keep the program fresh and effective.

WHAT TURNS "NEWS" INTO CONVERSATIONS?

Make it re-mark-able and people will likely remark on it!

What constitutes "news" is not a question that only confronts newspaper editors and TV news directors. It happens to all of us—whenever we sit down to transmit EMail messages, send out greeting cards, or write a letter. *News* is anything that can have a potential impact on our lives; gossip is something that entertains us in some way. The closer news comes to touching us or gossip comes to tickling us, the more we tend to talk about those items with others.

The other day an acquaintance returned from a holiday in Laughlin, Nevada. She had won $8,000 on a 25¢ progressive slot machine. I heard the news from my mother; I repeated it almost instantly to my brother and again to my wife. It provoked a lot of conversation—about the logistics of payment, about the taxes due, about what might be done with the money.

All that chatter about nothing that could benefit any of *us* personally made me think. What else causes that kind of spontaneous comment? When any person we know, event we attended, or place we visited is discussed in the media; certainly a wedding announcement or first pregnancy of a relative; perhaps an unexpected promotion, unwanted illness, or sudden accident befalling a friend. As one observer has noted: "...the purpose of news is no longer to provide knowledge, but to provide excitement...."

When a topic fails to attain this level of importance, a conversation about it has to be stimulated. People do not ordinarily go home to talk with their families or their friends about the speed of a dry cleaner, the generosity of a butcher, the kindness of an accountant, or the skill of a handyman. They do talk, however, when the product or the service is *unusual*—for good or bad. If it isn't "re-mark-able," then, it won't get talked about; it isn't news! The key, then, to generating word of mouth advertising is relatively simple—make what you do or what you say or what you offer DIFFERENT and people will likely talk about it to your benefit.

HOW TO CREATE A WORD OF MOUTH PROGRAM

As we have indicated, word of mouth programs begin when they are stimulated in some way. Take a Vietnamese hot sauce called *Sriracha*. It has become a huge success on the strength of friends *buying* bottles for others to try. The *Los Angeles Times* called it "word 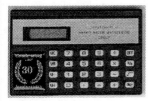 of (scorched) mouth." In another case, a calculator recently fell out of an envelope we opened. It was inscribed with the name and address of our consulting firm and decorated with a gold wreath proclaiming the celebration of our thirtieth year in business. It was such an impressive presentation that we showed it to the entire front office staff and we started to do exactly what the sponsoring company wanted us to do—think hard about their offer to buy fifty inscribed calculators for our clients.

Implementing a word of mouth program flows easily once the item that is to be used to get attention has been selected. If you are giving something away, make it unusual; if you are showing something, make it different; if you are offering something, make it noteworthy.

We were once asked to create a reason for people to visit a particular warm weather resort in the winter. We eventually suggested the community sponsor a Valentine's Week of street dances and other outdoor events. We reasoned that since no community celebrates Valentine's Day, let alone the whole week surrounding February 14, it could become a national focal point for the traditional day set aside to celebrate love. The idea was never launched because the community lacked the funds to organize the initial event. Shame. We thought the very freshness of the concept would be the spark for getting word of mouth to sustain the event over the years to follow.

A matter of presenting the unusual.

161

BODY LANGUAGE CAN BE AS EFFECTIVE AS WORDS IN CONVEYING INFORMATION

Remember that most film makers want their audiences to leave the theatre smiling— perhaps the single-most effective form of non-verbal communication.

As we have noted previously, most people consider word of mouth a verbal exercise. In fact, of course, a great deal of the advantages of word of mouth can be orchestrated by other verbal means—by letter, by poster, by bumper sticker, by EMail, and by a worldwide web site.

Word of mouth also occurs through body language— a thumbs up gesture, an okay signal, or a vigorous nod can all convey specific information about a product, service, or event that one person seeks from another.

A lot of *general* information can also be delivered by body language. I remember my father-in-law, Eddie Davidson, standing at the back of his swap meet spot. He sold mostly jeans and shirts at a substantial discount from traditional retail stores. He used to stand at the back so he could watch all the tables where his goods were laid out and direct his employees toward customers who needed assistance. He stood with his legs spread just beyond the width of his shoulders and his arms folded tightly across his chest. Anybody who saw him felt his confidence; this was a guy who was daring the world to find better quality goods at a lower price anywhere else. His body language suggested he did not want to debate the point. Interestingly, I always thought that if he had proclaimed that point on a banner or said it to shoppers as they passed by, he wouldn't have been nearly as effective. Unlike so many who oversell what they have, he never said a word; he allowed his physical demeanor and the goods themselves to tell the story he wanted to convey.

Anyone setting out to develop a word of mouth program needs to remember the simple point—it isn't so much *what* is said, but *how* it's said that will count the most.

PROVIDING THE WORDING FOR WORD OF MOUTH COMMENTS

When you provide the public with a means to generate word of mouth comments, be sure to give them some key phrases and selling arguments—a script—to pass along to their friends, colleagues, or contacts.

A few years ago, we suggested that a Los Angeles non-profit group offer pre-paid phone cards as a means of getting word of mouth started about its activities *and* raising funds. We also told the group that they should encourage phone card recipients to use the card to talk about their experiences while still enjoying their trip.

We encouraged the non-profit group to plant ideas in a message that would accompany the phone card. Here is how we phrased that message:

> *A Message from the Los Angeles County Music & Performing Arts Commission*
>
> To Old and New Friends:
>
> We hope that you are enjoying your current stay in the Los Angeles area and that you have had an opportunity to see some of the places that give this city and its surrounding communities their unique reputation. Like people everywhere, we are always curious about the places and events that make the biggest impression on our visitors—the moments that you will remember most vividly and that you will want to describe to your friends and family when you return home.
>
> If you have just arrived in the area or still have some time left, may we suggest places that we think you shouldn't miss.

Be sure to help those who you would like to help you.

Word of Mouth Pitch No. 1—Get Them to Think

163

WORD OF MOUTH TECHNIQUES

Word of Mouth
Pitch No. 2—
Remind Them
What They Can
Describe to the
People They Are
Calling

Most of these you will have seen on television or in the movies, but in person they make an even more lasting memory: The Hollywood Bowl, the Los Angeles Music Center, the Greek Theatre, the New Getty Museum, the Griffith Park Observatory, and many more. We also have a host of spectacular new facilities that you may not know much about—the Museum of Contemporary Art, the Fowler at UCLA, the Petersen Automotive Museum, the Museum of Tolerance, the Museum of Miniatures, and much more still. They are all worth your time.

Word of Mouth
Pitch No. 3—
Challenge Them
to Describe the
Don't Miss
Features of a Los
Angeles Visit.

We hope you put your Personal LA Telecom Calling Card to good use and that you will take time to tell your friends and family what they should be sure to see and do during *their* visit to Los Angeles in the years to come. And if you care to let us know some of your thoughts about Los Angeles, that would be very interesting for us as well.

Executive Director

When you get people to think about what they will say about a product, service, place, or event, you have created a more articulate and therefore more effective word of mouth advertising source.

THE WORD OF MOUTH ADVISOR

When Apple Computer announced that they had hired a new public relations agency and a new advertising agency to "complete" their new marketing team, we thought that Apple ought to also consider appointing a specialist to enlist its *customers* in the marketing effort. Here is the letter we sent to CEO Steve Jobs at Apple on our idea for a word of mouth advisor:

> **HARRIS/RAGAN MANAGEMENT GROUP**
>
> Dear Mr. Jobs:
>
> I could not help but note that [your new marketing] team lacked a *word of mouth advisor*. Not surprising, of course, since the position has not yet been invented. But...given the differences among traditional advertising efforts, public relations activities, and word of mouth comments, someone needs to take charge of developing favorable person-to-person comments. [N]o company has yet had the foresight to engage someone solely to develop word of mouth programs, but of all the world-class enterprises that might benefit most from a word of mouth advisor on its marketing team—given the renowned commitment and fierce loyalty of its customers—Apple stands almost alone.
>
> Unlike some marketing people, we do not believe that word of mouth advertising is a matter of random good fortune or something bestowed by the gossip gods. Rather, we believe that imaginative word of mouth programs can be nurtured and stimulated among customers to provide one of the most effective, least expensive forms of product promotion available.
>
> Sincerely,
>
> Godfrey Harris
> President

No one at Apple Computer bothered to acknowledge our letter, let alone respond to the concept. But the idea of an outside specialist to develop word of mouth programs at the same time more traditional advertising and public relations activities are under way still seems valid to us.

Include a word of mouth specialist with the PR and advertising agencies on your marketing team.

THE BEST SURPRISES EVOKE UNEXPECTED PLEASURE— AND THEN TALK

Discounts quietly accorded at the cash register may end up doing more good for a business than advertising the discount on a sign board.

A little while ago, an attorney went to a nursery close to his home to buy a bare root apricot tree to add to an "orchard" he was creating in his back yard. While at the nursery, he picked up a few other needed items— some fertilizer, plant food, a new pair of clippers. The entire bill came to around $50. The attorney handed the young cashier a Visa card. She peered at the picture on the card, then looked hard at the lawyer, and finally screwed up enough courage to ask his age. He is single now, but with two grown daughters. His mind whirled with all the possible implications of the question, but finally decided to be honest: "Sixty-two," he admitted. "Well, then," she said, "you are qualified for our 15 percent senior citizen discount."

He accepted the offer without comment. He hadn't known that this nursery offered special prices to senior citizens, and he doesn't often think of himself in the category of retirees. But when he got to the office the next day, he couldn't wait to tell his partner about the experience. It turns out he was more devastated by the offer than elated. He thinks of himself as still young, modern thinking, very eligible, and not beyond asking a thirty-something lady for a date. But *some* thirty-something ladies are apparently seeing him differently—as greying, slowing, and soon to be approaching the rocking chair at a nursing home.

One of the non-lawyers in the office overheard the conversation, but didn't want to get into a debate over whether the lawyer looked his age or not. He just wanted to know the exact location of the nursery. His wife, he said, does a lot of buying at nurseries, was born in the same year as the lawyer, and has never been offered a discount on her gardening purchases in her life. She is sure to want to go!

The word of mouth moral to this story is clear:

Never underestimate the power of surprise to generate conversation that may later bring new customers to your door.

IF YOU GOT IT, USE IT!

A few years ago, we were on a cruise ship of Panamanian registry. The ship was Italian in ownership, crew, and atmosphere and we were sailing in Canadian waters. In short, the Panamanian connection to the ship, save a small plaque near the bridge and the Panamanian flag flying over the stern, was a financial and legal convenience for its owners. Panamanian registry of merchant and resort ships, in fact, is so popular that the country claims the second largest ocean fleet in the world. The registry fees have become an important source of revenue for the country and keep its diplomats busy in various ports around the world.

Because of our long involvement with Panama, it occurred to us that the country's tourism industry ought to take advantage of the captive audience on cruise ships of Panamanian registry. We suggested that the government consider changing the registration rules to include a provision that all Panamanian ships carry a specified package of information about Panama. We had in mind the kind of basic information that encyclopedias list (people, geography, climate, history, government, transportation, natural resources, economy, etc.), that international accounting and law firms develop to describe the basic rules for doing business in a country and that is provided by tourism and convention authorities to prospective businesses on hotels, recreation facilities, meeting rooms, and so forth. We thought that the requirement was so innocuous that no shipping company would object, and we saw an enormous potential advantage to Panama in spreading word about its commercial and tourist attractions to people who were already disposed to visiting foreign places and dealing with foreign entities.

Every entity has supporters who can be used as word of mouth trumpets. At the least, nearly every business can call on a wife or husband, kids, parents, aunts, or uncles as couriers for business cards or brochures.

Take advantage of all the resources at your command to help build your business.

Some of them may also be able to arrange a social event or make a phone call for you. While some people are reluctant to recommend relatives for fear of losing a friend in the process, it usually turns out to be a favor to the person looking for some assistance with a problem or opportunity.

Every entity also has especially well satisfied customers—those who often profess that they don't know what they would do without the entity's being there to help. The next time you hear something like that ask the customer if he or she would be willing to help you expand your business. Depending on the response, any number of programs developed in this book might be employed to implement the offer.

The point is to use the resources you already have to expand your word of mouth reach; they are not only the cheapest form of promotion available, they are the most willing and by extension the most likely to succeed on your behalf. And always remember a litany we always repeat:

If you don't ask for what you want, how do you expect others to know what you want?

ANYTHING WORTH GIVING SHOULD BE GIVEN TWO FOLD

Most word of mouth promotion relies on the customer's being able to *describe to someone else* what he or she liked about a product, service, or event. Two-fer programs are much more direct—the customer is provided with an actual example of a product to give to someone else to experience.

Because this technique is designed to create a chain marketing reaction, all two-fer items should also be packaged with a coupon, discount order blank, or notice to permit those farther out on the chain to obtain an additional example to give to someone else.

We have described a two-fer program for publishers, and we suggest others for restauranteurs and retailers. We believe the concept of providing two of something is a fundamental word of mouth technique and should be factored into all word of mouth cost considerations.

The same goes for all special events you arrange for clients. Instead of a sales manager taking a customer to a baseball game or asking the customer to join the manager at a concert, have the client choose one of *his* or *her* customers to share the baseball game or an evening at a concert. The customer will enjoy the moment of being seen as generous, and the recipient of the invitation will be sure to ask about how the tickets were obtained.

Will the client take sole credit for the tickets and fail to promote the sponsoring company? Perhaps, but remember that all sides want results in order to repeat the experience in the future. Thus, there is a built-in incentive to pay proper homage to the sponsoring company.

> Two-fers are items presented in pairs— one for the customer to use and the other to be given away by the customer.

ACKNOWLEDGE EVERYTHING
CUSTOMERS DO FOR A BUSINESS

Acknowledging what customers do for a business builds loyalty and promotes confidence to speak about the business.

In the old days, *Life Magazine* made it a practice to acknowledge every individual who took the time to write a letter commenting on a published item—whether the editors intended to print the comment in a subsequent issue or not. By the same token, President Reagan's White House used to thank every person who wrote to him with a compliment, a complaint, or a comment. It wasn't elaborate—a simple pre-printed card with a replica signature—but it was gracious. It was also an *acknowledgment* that the person counted, that his or her opinion had worth, and that the President appreciated a citizen's effort to communicate a feeling, a fact, a problem, or a need. The Clinton White House can't seem to be bothered. Send a letter to this President, and if the staff doesn't recognize a name or a connection, it seems to disappear into the black hole of Presidential files. How does that make someone feel, particularly when the letter might be a response to the President's public solicitation for fresh ideas? We know. We felt foolish when we were suckered into responding to a Clinton appeal and then ignored.

An upset voter is not as significant, perhaps, as a disaffected customer. The *Harvard Woman's Health Watch* lost a subscriber when its editor failed to acknowledge a letter. The editor wrote: "[because]...the volume of surface and e-mail is large, we are usually able to answer only the mail that requires action, such as requests for information or complaints. We have assumed complimentary letters, like personal thank-you notes, don't require a response." They were wrong; they do. Staying in touch spreads good will and prevents bad feelings from spreading!

The White House and the *Harvard Woman's Health Watch* are not alone in forgetting the hand that feeds them. Oprah Winfrey regularly fails to acknowledge the fans that write to show their appreciation for a segment or a particular program. Pretty soon these faithful fans can feel betrayed; their loyalty may wither and their attention may be directed elsewhere. So, too, with *The Washington Monthly*. This respected political journal continually asks its readers to feed it fodder for its famous "Memo of the Month" feature—where the foibles of bureaucracy can be exposed—and to provide it with fresh observations for its "Tidbits & Outrages" page—where the eccentricities of modern life can be explored. Despite this reliance on readers to do at least some of its research, the *Monthly* never acknowledges its contributors—either in the magazine itself or privately. We have had two contributions published: One noted the delicious irony that a Ms. Black handled paid obituary announcements for the *Los Angeles Times* and a second that reported the campaign against drinking and driving has never seemingly reached the authorities in New Hampshire where state liquor stores are open long hours and thriving alongside the well-traveled interstate highways.

Would some form of pre-printed acknowledgment or some sign of appreciation for a contribution from Charles Peters, the editor, be so burdensome on the magazine? Might the payoff, in terms of increased submissions and expanded attention to the journal, be worth the few dollars and staff time that might be involved? It seems to us that saying thank you to volunteers is not only a matter of common courtesy, it is also a matter of smart business. The loss of potential favorable word of mouth advertising seems particularly wasteful when people are ignored. We think pride of recognition would generate animated and broad-based talk among family and friends. This kind of talk, amplified to acquaintances and contacts, is the basis for building and broadening a reputation and strengthening market position at virtually no cost. Just as Oprah needs strong ratings, so *The Washington Monthly* needs consistent circulation. The easiest way to develop both is through favorable word of mouth commentary from fans and readers. Ignoring them creates the breeding ground for negative word of mouth comments if a fan or reader turns hostile.

If we had to give just one piece of advice to all start-ups and small businesses concerning how to create word of mouth comments, it would be this: *Acknowledge everything a customer does to support your enterprise—from giving you a sale, to making a comment, to bringing in a friend.* Like a locomotive leaving a train station, word of mouth starts slowly before it can gain speed. Acknowledging the contributions of customers is the first step in developing the momentum that will sustain any business in bad patches and allow it to grow in good times.

If location, location, location is the mantra of sound real estate investment, then *acknowledge, acknowledge, acknowledge* has to be the key to developing positive word of mouth commentary.

SURPRISE THEM WITH SOMETHING OUT OF THE ORDINARY

A little shock value also has surprise value.

We can't say often enough that surprising consumers has great value in sparking word of mouth commentary. If it blends in with everything else, people may see it, but it does not make a sufficient impression to cause comment. If it is surprisingly different, it becomes remarkable in every sense of that word.

Take a long straight residential street in Los Angeles, with expensive houses on either side. Trees dot the lawns; mail boxes stand sentry at the curbs. As we drove this street some two months before the last U.S. Presidential election, we saw something new, something seemingly out of place among the pristine flower beds and well trimmed hedges. It was a sign announcing that that particular house supported Brad Sherman for Congress!

We had no idea who he was or why anyone would support him. We bet that of the thousands of cars that passed the house in subsequent days, few could have told you Mr. Sherman's political party, let alone anything about his background or program. In a forest of campaign posters, no one would have noticed the Sherman name. But when there were no other political signs visible, the one promoting Mr. Sherman's candidacy provoked curiosity, attention, and later recognition.

We noticed it; we think others must have too. The sign didn't give us any information, other than the fact that Mr. Sherman was a candidate for Congress. But it was enough to make those who noticed it read the next article that appeared in the paper or mailer that arrived at the house.

Did the surprise value of that isolated sign work? We can't say for sure—and probably not on its own—but we do know that Mr. Sherman's first run for public office was successful.

MAKE 'EM CURIOUS

Some time ago we were driving through Beverly Hills, California, when we started to see blue ribbons wrapped around trees, blue wreaths on the front gates of homes, blue ribbons on public buildings. We saw them, but we didn't understand their significance. So we began asking around—friends, merchants, others. What do all these blue ribbons signify?

It wasn't long before we had an answer. They indicated support of the police. The homes, the offices, and the buildings were showing their appreciation for the work of the local police force.

A nice tribute we thought, but also a terrific way to encourage people to talk about a product, service, or event. It could work for any business or organization at any time. Try it with any symbol or mark that comes to mind. Make the symbol or mark visible around job sites, company facilities, or on personnel, and people will soon become curious enough to try to find out the meaning.

Another example of the power of curiosity occurred a few years ago with the film, *The Crying Game*. The producers even captured the phenomenon in their advertisements with the words: "The movie everyone is talking about, but no one is giving away its secrets." That was true. The film contained a stunning scene that surprised everyone who saw it; people came away telling others they *had* to see the movie, but without revealing the special moment.

Provide people with a colored ribbon, a lapel pin, a slogan—something that draws attention and makes people curious—and then listen to them start a conversation about it.

> If people have to ask about something, talk has already started.

ALWAYS OFFER AN INCENTIVE

Reward those whom you ask to speak for you.

Some months ago we heard a radio advertisement urging listeners to call their cable company to ask that a new network be added to the others already presented to subscribers of the cable service. The announcer urged listeners to call the following number to learn more about what the new network would be offering:

1 800 FX FX FX FX.

Properly excited, the announcement then charged listeners with the responsibility of calling their cable company to tell them it was wanted.

As soon as we heard the ad for the first time, we knew we had been given a classic example of how *not* to do a word of mouth program. First of all, nearly everybody who listens to radio today is doing something else—driving a car, walking the dog, working in the garden, stocking a shelf. Almost no one listens with a pad and pencil handy to write down whatever it is they are being told. So remembering exactly how many FX's to punch in would have been a challenge. But more importantly, the cable company was asking the listener to do *two* things for it—listen to a further promotion on the phone, then make the call to the local cable company. Think about it! Do you know many people who would voluntarily undertake this sort of task without an incentive?

Common sense suggests that if you want people to talk about your product or service, you have to offer them some kind of reward to do so. We don't know how many people actually did as they were asked in that radio ad. However, we would bet response would have been improved had the sponsors offered a free video cassette with sample original programming as the starting point for people to become interested enough to want to call their cable company—with appropriate telephone and fax numbers, EMail and snail mail addresses provided in a cover letter.

GET THEM WONDERING

When we saw an advertisement for a new movie in a newspaper a while ago, we fell in love with the word of mouth potential of its explanatory banner line:

The ad clearly provoked a thought about what was *the* most outrageous trial of the century. A horde of answers flooded through our mind: The OJ Simpson trial in Los Angeles, the Manuel Noriega trial in Miami, the Rodney King beating trial in Simi Valley? No right answer here, but certainly a lot of fodder for thought and discussion. In the same vein, a Los Angeles restaurant proudly proclaims that it serves the city's *second* best chili. Doesn't that make you curious as to who they think is ahead of them?

If you can't surprise your customers into talking about you, you can certainly peak their curiosity or challenge potential customers to find out something for themselves.

Get the conversation started yourself with a statement that begs for discussion.

AVOID FALLING INTO THE FAKE WORD OF MOUTH TRAP

Be aware of the style of phony word of mouth programs.

As we have noted before, the power of word of mouth advertising is recognized by all marketing people, even if almost all of them don't really grasp the essentials of the concept. As a result, marketing channels are clogged with fake endorsements, phony referrals, actors performing as ordinary citizens, and assorted other tricks to lead potential customers to think that a particular product or service has been voluntarily and independently supported by a friend or neighbor. Here is a short check list of items NOT to use in creating your own word of mouth program for fear of having them taken as a fake:

- **Avoid broad categories.** Many advertisers use occupations to indicate support. "Truckers say..." or "Nurses tell their friends..." or "Doctors recommend..." These phrases certainly start to sound like word of mouth, but are clearly not.

- **Don't use initials.** We received a fax recently asking us to read what people are supposed to be saying about a weight loss program:

  T.M. of Albuquerque: I won't starve myself to lose weight. With Slender Now, I don't have to.

  or

  G.K. of Columbia, TN: My first 13 days I lost 8 pounds.

  While these comments may have been excerpted from real letters, the reader doesn't know the individuals and, as a result, cannot put the thoughts into a personal context that is an essential of word of mouth advertising.

- **Never offer money.** Many companies hoping for a referral offer customers sums of money *if* the person referred becomes a customer. These programs smack of putting customers in the position of *selling* their friends. It is not only demeaning to most, it changes word of mouth from being based on trust to being based on profit.

GETTING IT RIGHT!

Two of the firms on our floor received the same Christmas gift from the same talent agency; we noticed them early one morning because they had been left unwrapped at the front door of each suite. They were mouse pads tucked into colorful holiday bags. What made them so impressive and so special was the care with which the information on the pads had been created and presented.

The mouse pad had a telephone directory printed on it, but the numbers were organized and categorized into an amusing, artful, and comprehensive package for Hollywood's most powerful people. "CAN'T FIND A NUMBER? WITH GOLD/MARSHAK/LIEDTKE ON YOUR DESK, THERE'S NO NEED TO WONDER!" the headline said. Marching down the four colums were listings for the headquarters of the unions, legitimate theatres, studios, various major theatre complexes, airlines and taxi companies, messenger and delivery services, hotels, restaurants, clubs—in short the essential contact points for anyone in the fast lane. We don't think it was all serious. Under *Health & Services*, listed telephone numbers included Cedars Sinai Medical Center and Over-Eaters Anonymous, as well as the Suicide Prevention Hotline and Forest Lawn Cemetery. Under the category *Great Talent*, the only listing was the name and telephone number of the pad's creator and sponsor: Gold/Marshak/Liedtke.

Oh, we could have nit-picked the list—no flower or bookstores were mentioned; no referral services (yellow page directory assistance, police emergency) were given. The mouse pad information was not copyrighted, and the categories were not in alphabetical order. Had they provided more than one to each recipient—for the recipient to give to someone else in the industry—they might have spread their name and advertised their creativity beyond their immediate client list. But these thoughts are all small change. Gold/Marshak/Leidtke created a basis for people to be in touch with them and, they created a network of contacts among

The right gift will always encourage word of mouth.

the firms listed to help build their reputation.

Now, stop for a moment. If you consider yourself the best in what you do—whatever that is—start putting down the supportive and peripheral companies that are involved in your field that you could list in a similar approach. Whatever list you develop, it need not be reproduced on a mousepad, but could be used as the header for a calendar, in a fold-out for a glove compartment directory, on a computer disk, at the top of a scratch pad, and so on.

Others have done things that knowingly or unknowingly enhance the word of mouth about their products, services, businesses, and events. Here is a potpourri that we have recently come across:

- **Six Flags Magic Mountain** got it exactly right, in our view, with a promotion they ran last summer. They sent out discount passes to corporations in a strip of six. Each pass was valid for up to six general use tickets obtained from the box office at the time of entry. Each offered a variety of discounts depending on the day and season of use. The tickets had a seven-month shelf life and were both colorfully printed and informative about the facilities, times of operation, and special programs being planned. We never used the tickets ourselves, but we did send a few to clients and gave the balance to our staff. They made us look generous and important to people who could help us in the future.

- **Stephen Fossler Company**, makers of self-sticking foil seals to help businesses celebrate major anniversaries, has long had it right. The Chicago-area company not only sells something that provides an instant word of mouth story, but sends customers the 10-percent overruns produced for *free* and encloses a book—*Fossler's Guide to Planning and Promoting Your Anniversay*—with each order.

- **A Lexus dealer** in Northern California challenged a radio audience with words to the effect that buying this car at this dealership is no ordinary experience. "That's right," the announcer said, "you'll be so impressed you'll actually mention the experience to your friends." While setting expectations so high is always dangerous—disappointment can trigger negative word of mouth faster than pleasure promotes positive comments—we liked the idea of getting customers to focus on their response to the experience *before* they actually encountered it.

- Many years ago, **TEXACO** ran a contest: "Write Your Own TV Commercial." Each contestant received a letter that said with so "many interesting commercials...the judging will be difficult." Winners, the letter promised, would be notified by mail. "Please accept the enclosed TEXACO Road Atlas as a token of appreciation for your participation in the contest." It was unexpected. It was unannounced, and it was as impressive as it was inexpensive. It made contestants friends of Texaco for life.

- **Orion Classics,** a film distributor specializing in foreign films, came close to developing a word of mouth program that we would have endorsed, but fell just short. Instead of offering exiting audience members special discount coupons for tickets to subsequent showings of the *same* film— to give to their friends, relatives, and colleagues as an inexpensive way of continuation marketing—Orion employees were offering passes to a totally different film on a specific day at a specific time a week away. Glowing with enjoyment at the film just seen, most wanted to talk about its special qualities, not whether arrangements could be made to see a different movie at a different time on a different day. Few people bothered to take the passes offered.

- **Jack Chapman** has written a book entitled, *Negotiating Your Salary: How to Make $1000 a Minute.* It was ordered by a colleague of ours directly from the publisher. The book itself came with a letter from the author that asked our colleague for "a favor." The author explained that bookstores tend to bump his book in favor of the newest, most up-to-date, expanded title on other self-help topics for business people. "IF (*sic*) you like this book, and feel that you would recommend it to clients or friends of yours, could you please help us make it readily available to them? Here's all you'd have to do. Sign and mail the enclosed letter (we've put it on your 'letterhead') to a local bookstore. (If we know the address of one in your area, we've already entered that address; otherwise, maybe you'll know of one yourself. Thanks a lot." The enclosed letter, identifying the name and mailing address of the sender, plus his telephone number, was addressed: "Dear Bookstore Buyer." It said: "I recently purchased *Negotiating Your Salary*...by mail because I did not see it in the CAREERS section in your store. I will be recommending it to some friends of mine and would like to be able to refer them to your store. Could you please order a couple of copies? I would appreciate it." We don't know if the techniques have increased sales, but we do know that author Jack Chapman and Ten Speed Press are on the right track when it comes to generating word of mouth advertising.

Alcoa Chief Executive Paul O'Neill refused to allow his company to participate in political fund raising. He said: "Once we got the question right [do we want to be part of a system in which the only way to get representation is to buy it?], the answer was easy. No." So, too, with word of mouth. Once you understand how people react to your products or services, designing a program to amplify that reaction is easy.

HOW WOULD YOU REACT?

Some attempts at word of mouth advertising probably have no real impact.

We rented a film called *Marvin's Room* to watch at home. As we pulled the cassette from its jacket, we noted that Miramax, its distributor, had printed a command on the videotape label: "Recommend This Movie to Friends." The suggestion was printed in a typeface about the same size as that used to name the stars of the film: Meryl Streep, Leonardo DiCaprio, Diane Keaton, and Robert DeNiro.

While the film was interesting, the label was fascinating. In our view it was a nice try at word of mouth, but not something we would recommend. It is probably the result of someone in the Miramax marketing department trying to stimulate word of mouth about the film. Had they read this book or either of its two predecessors—*Talk Is Cheap* and *How to Generate Word of Mouth Advertising*—they would have realized that commanding people to do something probably won't work. If people like a movie, they may tell their friends about it and urge them to rent it—whatever a label on the cassette suggested. If they don't like a film, that kind of urging will have no impact on them and might even evoke a sarcastic negative response such as, "Oh, sure!"

Had we been asked how to make something like the label message effective, we might have suggested that a secret question be imbedded at the end of the tape. Anyone answering the question and submitting a response to the distributor would receive a discount coupon from the distributor for a subsequent rental—the same title or another. That kind of quiz might just be the kind of incentive that could get a renter to encourage a friend to see the film and confirm the color of the actress's dress, the use of a word by one of the actors, or some other arcane detail of the film. Another thought: Rather than the imperious command to "Recommend This Movie to Friends!" we might suggest a challenge to the viewer: "Which of Your Friends Would Appreciate This Movie?" Our view is that if you get them thinking, they may soon be *talking*.

BEING TOO CLEVER BY HALF
CAN CAUSE A
NEGATIVE REACTION

The world of direct marketing is now filled with people selling multi-colored envelopes designed to look like the covers used for Priority Mail or Federal Express. The people selling envelopes to those in multi-level marketing pitch the theme that the envelope will improve the chances that the piece will be opened and its contents considered by the recipient. We don't know whether the claim is true, but it seems a harmless play on some recognizable symbols.

Not so with those who attempt to *fool* recipients into thinking that they are someone else. Look at the logo below for the giant American Association of Retired Persons.

Now look at the logo on envelopes used by a private company that calls itself the Association of Affiliated Financial Professionals.

As far as we know, the AARP has nothing to do with the AAFP, but we suspect that the latter does not mind if recipients of its mailing pieces think there might be a connection. But we see a big difference between fake express envelopes and an imitative logo. In the first case, the contents have no relationship to the look of the envelope; in the latter case, the contents discuss financial subjects that could well be within the interest of the American Association of Retired Persons and therefore could be resented.

If you have something worthwhile to sell, sell it on its merits and what it will do for the prospective customer. If it does what it purports to do, the customer will be only too happy to talk about it with others. But if buyers discover that the seller is trying to fool them—or they end up buying something under false pretenses—then the negative word of mouth can do much more damage than any good to be potentially derived.

> Trying to fool people can backfire into a stream of negative word of mouth.

TAKE CARE ON THE INTERNET

As useful as the medium is to communicate, it also has the power to enrage.

We have already noted the terrific power of EMail and WEB sites to communicate factual information about a product, service, business, or event. Over the last 1000 or so years, the marketplace has changed dramatically. What started out in open areas around town squares later moved indoors to the ground floor of homes. Eventually, these specialty stores gave way to the general store, the department store, and, finally, the shopping mall. Merchandising then modernized once again as mail order and TV shopping networks were invented. Now the vast worldwide reach of the Internet may become the newest marketing medium.

As effective as one-on-one word of mouth conversation can be as a means of promotion for any product, service, event or business, nothing touches the sheer power of one message being passed to dozens—even tens of thousands of dozens—of people across the Internet. But there are some major cautions to note when creating word of mouth programs that stimulate customers into using the Internet as a means of "talking" about your product, service, event, or business.

- EMail cannot convey voice modulation or the exquisite detail of body language; speaking softly or forcefully about a product or showing excitement through the eyes or hands is clearly lost in electrical transmission. As pointed out before (see pp. 16-17), keyboard symbols prove poor substitutes for the real thing.

- While words are said to count for only 7-percent of the message transmitted in face-to-face conversations, their effect obviously zooms in Internet communication. As a result, before suggesting any wording for a written communication, be sure to test the words. Write them down, print them out, and give them to a number of people to read. Ask for impressions—what they got out of the message, what action they were supposed to take, what questions the message raised, and so forth.

- People have become inundated with spammed EMail—junk electronic letters sent out by companies to a vast array of addressees unknown to the sender. If you provide something that you intend to end up on EMail, make sure it gets personalized by the sender before it is dispatched over the Internet.

- People have also been taken in by a vast array of EMail messages that purport to report the truth, but are really only intended as a bit of humor. Many other cases are exercises in ego—to demonstrate the prowess of the sender in stirring reaction—or disinformation—to harm the subject of the message. Here are just a few examples of this phenomena:

  + A message that recently raced around the world several times was a college commencement speech attributed to author Kurt Vonnegut. It contained a lot of very amusing pieces of wisdom for graduates:

    * "Dance, even if you have nowhere to do it but your living room."

    * "Be kind to your knees. You'll miss them when they're gone."

    * "Keep your old love letters. Throw away your old bank statements."

    Mr. Vonnegut did not write the piece nor deliver the address. Rather, the "address" first appeared as a column in a Boston newspaper. It was as if one person passed the column to another with a comment that it *sounds* like something Kurt Vonnegut might have written. Several relays later, the "sounds like something" got lost and an Internet legend was born.

  + Another cybermyth involved the clothing designer Tommy Hilfiger. Hilfiger supposedly appeared on a CNN style segment and said that he didn't think Asians looked good in his clothes. Then the story morphed. No, it wasn't CNN and it wasn't Asians; it was said on the Oprah Winfrey Show about African Americans, and she threw him off the set. Hilfiger never appeared on either program. The same myth struck Liz Claiborne who supposedly told Oprah on the air that she only designs for white people. Spike Lee fell in and even was quoted in *Esquire* as saying: "It definitely happened. Get the tape." It didn't, and the tape doesn't exist.

To prevent your EMail word of mouth message from being distorted or trashed or even becoming a cybermyth, always provide alternate points of contact/information in your message—telephone or fax number, web site, snail mail address, or other identifying material.

TESTING YOUR
WORD OF MOUTH IQ

Redo your promo- tional material with a word of mouth flair!

All commercial art students have had the assignment: Take something very familiar and very ordinary and create new packaging that maintains the item's original functions, but gives the product a fresh feel.

Take menorahs, the Jewish ceremonial candlelabra at the center of Channukah celebrations. The next time you are in a store that sells Judaica, be sure to look at the dozens of interpretations artists keep giving to how the eight Channukah candles can be displayed. By the same token, note the number of interpretations—on book covers, government documents, newspaper illustrations, and the like—that the fifteen gold stars and blue field of the European Union flag spark to convey "European-ness." Try watch and clock faces, even binoculars. Nearly every art student has been asked to draw a different way to present these common objects.

Rethinking something that is very familiar holds just as true for marketing. Now that you are at the end of this book, look at the promotional material in use for your business with fresh eyes. Rather than merely updating a piece for price, dates, or features, why not try to re-create it with some form of word of mouth appeal. It will test how well you have internalized the principles advocated in this book and might give you some terrific new ways to boost your sales with new approaches.

As you rethink your presentation and products, ask yourself:

- Will it provoke a conversation?
- Will people know what to say on your behalf?
- Will people be positive in their attitude?
- Will you be prepared for the benefits to come?

NOTES

CONCLUSION

Several years ago, Fletcher Jones, Jr., bought a copy of our book, *Talk Is Cheap*. Mr. Jones not only possesses one of the legendary names in Southern California—his father is forever associated with the sale of Chevrolets in the area—but he himself owns a major Mercedes Benz dealership in Newport Beach. Recently, his dealership opened a spectacular new $15 million facility to sell new and used cars and to provide servicing. The facility not only has a luxurious waiting room for patrons, but includes computer-ready work stations, a children's play area, and a putting green. It even offers it own brand of bottled water to its "guests" (as customers are called) and to its "team members" (as employees are referred to.) The first lesson of word of mouth advertising is to do something *remarkable* enough to cause people to talk about your product or business. The lessons from *Talk Is Cheap* seem to have had an impact on his attitude toward business. In fact, he has done so much that people cannot help but talk about the experience of doing business with his dealership.

If doing something remarkable is the first lesson in word of mouth advertising, then the last lesson involves being silent about what may have been done to stimulate it. This is admittedly a strange form of non-sequitur—urging people to promote talk but not talk about it themselves! With most people believing that word of mouth happens by chance, anything that seems to stimulate conversation about a product, service, or event may be seen as manipulative. Some people inadvertently involved in such programs may feel used or sullied when they learn that someone created the circumstances or products to encourage talk. Those feelings can cause negative comments. As a result, many of the most successful word of mouth programs are the ones that do not appear to have been orchestrated or even chronicled. For people who make their living suggesting how talk can be beneficial, urging silence about the results of their most successful work products is admittedly very difficult.

Difficult or not, it will have to be done for a few more years until the business schools and major commercial organizations accept the fact that word of mouth is a different form of marketing and every bit as legitimate as traditional media advertising, public relations, and product presentation in the promotion of goods and services.

We believe it—and now that you have completed this book, we hope you do, too!

THE NATIONAL
WORD OF MOUTH REGISTER

The National Word of Mouth Register is currently in the development stage. It is seen by the author's consulting firm as a formal way to generate positive word of mouth comments about a product or service and get negative word of mouth feelings out in the open. Businesses who participate in the Register will receive a supply of individualized REGISTER FORMS (see example on the following page). Each form will be a postage paid postcard, designed to be stacked near cash registers in a retail store, placed on the bill tray at restaurants, or slipped in with a mailed invoice. The form would invite customers to let the Register know the good and bad points about a business and/or its products or services.

Businesses will be able to acquire the forms for free and customers will be able to make their comments for free. The Register will organize the incoming data in convenient categories—name of business, location, type of product or service, and so forth—and would provide the rating information gathered to any business or member of the general public for a small fee.

Like the famous published Zagat Surveys of restaurants—a systematic way to allow the general public to comment on food establishments in various communities—the National Word of Mouth Register would be an institutionalized way to allow companies to use positive word of mouth comments to build business and correct situations that create negative word of mouth that hurt business.

The word of mouth reports will be promoted through advertising, public relations, and, of course, word of mouth itself. In the latter case, we envisage arming every participant—those who send in cards and those who request information—with a special information packet to pass along to *their* colleagues, associates, friends, and relatives about the National Word of Mouth Register.

For more information on the National Word of Mouth Register, please contact:

National Word of Mouth Register
c/o Harris/Ragan Management Group
9200 Sunset Blvd., Suite 404
Los Angeles, CA 90069-3506 USA

or visit:

www.wordofmouthregister.com

The National Word of Mouth Register

ENTER NAME OF PRODUCT, SERVICE, OR BUSINESS HERE:

Put Your Rating in the Appropriate Box Below According to the Following Scale:

-5	-4	-3	-2	-1	0	+1	+2	+3	+4	+5
		Below Expectation			Met Expectation			Exceeded Expectation		

THIS PRODUCT, SERVICE, OR BUSINESS CONSISTENTLY

☐ **EXCEEDS MY EXPECTATIONS?**

☐ **MEETS MY EXPECTATIONS?**

☐ **FALLS BELOW MY EXPECTATIONS?**

THE DATA FROM THIS AND LIKE FORMS WILL BE COMPILED AND PROVIDED UNDER CERTAIN CONDITIONS TO OTHERS. ALL NAMES, RATINGS, AND COMMENTS WILL BE KEPT STRICTLY CONFIDENTIAL.

Please Tell Us the Things You Like About This Business and/or Its Product/Services

Please Tell Us What You Think Could Be Improved About This Business and/or Its Product/Services

Please Tell Us the Things You Don't Like About This Business and/or Its Product/Services

THE FOLLOWING INFORMATION IS FOR USE OF THE WORD OF MOUTH REGISTER TO CONFIRM INFORMATION ABOUT A PRODUCT, SERVICE OR BUSINESS AND WILL NOT BE DIVULGED

Name

Mailing Address

City, State/Province, Postal Code

Country

Telephone or FAX number,, or Email Address, in case verification is necessary.

Management Group. All Rights Reserved. 1998

FRONT

Word of Mouth Register
9200 Sunset Blvd., Suite 404
Los Angeles, CA 90069-3506
(800) 966-7716

NO POSTAGE
NECESSARY
IF MAILED
IN THE
UNITED
STATES

BUSINESS REPLY MAIL

FIRST CLASS MAIL   PERMIT NO. XXXXX   LOS ANGELES, CA

POSTAGE WILL BE PAID BY ADDRESSEE

Word of Mouth Register
9200 Sunset Blvd., Suite 404
Los Angeles, CA 90069

BACK

ACKNOWLEDGMENTS

Nancy B. Art

Nancy is an editor who tells us what she thinks of our syntax, grammar, and organizational skills and then corrects everything she finds wrong. Any errors that may be found are not her fault, but either our stubbornness in not accepting her recommendations or sloppiness in not making a change.

William P. Butler

Bill Butler was the first person I told about the assignment to do a paper on word of mouth advertising. We have subsequently worked together on trying to use word of mouth techniques to gain greater appreciation of the fact that union work produces better quality rather than just higher prices.

Gregrey J Harris

Greg is the author's eldest son and co-author of two predecessor books: *Talk is Cheap* and *How to Generate Word of Mouth Advertising*. While family obligations and business responsibilities did not give him sufficient free time to join in this project, this book would not have been possible without his previous contributions.

Barbara D. Mayer

Barbara is the author's wife and has contributed so much to this and the previous word of mouth books through her patience, readings, and discussions. She is particularly to be thanked for the Fedoskino story and the analogy to Moscow's 850th Anniversary.

James F. Ragan, Jr.

Jim is the Ragan of Harris/Ragan, a former partner who now heads his own consulting firm specializing in public involvement in public policy issues. He also teaches negotiations at a graduate business school. He provided us with the terrific example of how an author has used word of mouth techniques to get his book carried in bookstores and read by others.

John Roberts

We discussed several of our word of mouth ideas with John Roberts, the proprietor of an exquisite optical boutique in Beverly Hills. His reaction to the ideas, as well as his perceptive views on a number of other topics, were greatly appreciated.

Guillermo de St. Malo A.

A prominent Panamanian involved in US/Panamanian relations before the United States invasion reported the information on the political importance of word of mouth commentary in his country.

Desiree Vidal

Desiree works for The Americas Group and assisted with various aspects of the book that required extra research and verifications.

INDEX